When We Pray

When We Pray

A Prayer Journal for Pastors and Worship Leaders

Year A

Bob and Lavon Bayler

United Church Press
Cleveland, Ohio

United Church Press, Cleveland, Ohio 44115

Printed in the United States of America on acid-free paper
00 99 98 97 96 95   5 4 3 2 1

Library of Congress Cataloging-in-Publication Data

Bayler, Lavon, 1933–
       When we pray : a prayer journal for pastors and worship leaders / Lavon and Bob Bayler.
              p.   cm.
       Includes index.
       ISBN 0-8298-1103-6 (alk. paper)
       1. Church year—Prayer-books and devotions—English. 2. Pastoral prayers. 3. Common lectionary (1992) I. Bayler, Bob, 1934– . II. Title.
       BV30.B39   1995
       264'.13—dc20   94-39950
                                                                                          CIP

Honoring

faithful and competent

secretaries

who have assisted us

in our ministry;

currently:

Ruth Roche

and

Inge Bisanz

and, through the years:

Aretta, Barb, Brenda, Connie,

Dorothy, Frances, Gloria, Jan, Joyce,

Martha, Mary, Pat, and Sharon—

Thanks . . .

Contents

Foreword

Ten years ago, when my sabbatical project was to prepare a book of worship resources based on the ecumenical lectionary, I could not have imagined the extent of the task I was undertaking. One book demanded two more, eked out in the early morning devotional times and dominating every vacation. Then the three-year cycle of reading was updated to become the *Revised Common Lectionary*. The changes were extensive enough to suggest either considerable revisions to what I had previously written or entirely new responses to the texts. I chose the latter. A new series of three books was needed.

Meanwhile, another request was being resisted. Several persons inquired about the possibility of longer "pastoral prayers" related to the lectionary. Our hesitation to respond came largely from a concern that such prayers be contextual, emerging primarily out of immediate situations, not just echoing the scriptures. Then my husband, Bob, agreed to assist me with the project. A workbook format would encourage users of our books to edit and add to prayers the pastoral concerns of the moment. Furthermore, the prayers could be an aid to personal devotions.

The first book in this new series, *When We Pray*, was based on the reading for Year B in the *Revised Common Lectionary*. I became the project manager, with Bob as a contributing writer. The current volume, *When We Pray, Year A*, centering on the "year of Matthew," is Bob's project, to which I have contributed. Amid major transitions in our working lives, it has been good to find respite in the times of prayer to which our United Church Press editors kept recalling us. We listened to each other, occasionally making suggestions. As we look ahead to the third book in this series, we have invited colleagues to join us in the endeavor.

May all our prayers be more than words. As we open ourselves to the Eternal One, our longings and our listening draw us into a community of caring. When we pray, our lives are changed for the better. Toward that end we offer this modest collection.

Lavon Bayler

Preface

Praying the scriptures requires an act of faith and hope. It is an act because it calls forth an active engagement with the texts. Each text of the *Revised Common Lectionary* demands faithful reflection on the context of its origin and on its informing power in our current lives. Many prayers in *When We Pray, Year A* attempt to engage origin and contemporary struggle in conversation with each other. Scripture lessons are not a static literature wherein we select an old familiar theme which fits the occasion for our praying or preaching. Rather, the lessons are a living focus of encounter with the Holy One who passionately beckons us to faithfully struggle with God's presence and with our Savior's life of compassionate service. We believe the lectionary texts actively engage our conceptual ability, our compassionate hearts, and our spiritual commitment to the One who claims our faithfulness to the Word made flesh.

Writing prayers which seek to be informed by lectionary texts is a journey of active faith. Indeed, praying is an act of faith. Through our praying, we actively engage our awareness that the Creator who gave us the breath of life continually sustains our lives. By praying with our minds, hearts, spirits, and voices, we acknowledge that surely the Creator of all life is working, through all the concrete relationships which impact our lives, to renew each life and to support it on its journey through the day. Many individuals and groups may observe or participate in the same circle of relationships without seeing or believing that a divine presence is there to transform the day. Lifting up the dynamics of the day in prayers rooted in the lectionary texts is an act of faith. The texts beckon us to see the day, the people, the creatures, the relationships, the work, the play, the city, the town, and the world as occasions where God comes to visit us. When we pray in faith, God's presence appears.

Yet we would not pray at all if we were not energized by an act of hope. Deep down, when we pray there is a sense of anticipation. There is, however faintly felt, a vision of a way to overcome disappointment. There is, however desperate the struggle, a certainty that we shall overcome. And there is a sense of solidarity with all those who commit themselves to make the text live in the day's deeds. Writing prayers grounded in lectionary texts is an exercise in hope. The texts force us to engage them with hope. Working with them is an anticipation that we will discover the Creator's hopeful word for the day. There are some times when you may wonder whether any good word from the Holy One will be given through the lectionary lessons before you. We have found our engagement with the texts to be an opportunity to see the Bible's wealth of language as a call to prayer.

When We Pray, Year A is the fruit of engaging lectionary texts as a source for crafting prayers. Yet it is more than that. It is faith and hope expressed in the presence of God who calls faithful people to live through the text.

Bob Bayler

The Advent Season

Reflections

First Sunday of Advent

ISAIAH 2:1–5   ROMANS 13:11–14
PSALM 122   MATTHEW 24:36–44

Much of our lives, gracious God, is caught in the webs of night. Our private and communal conduct is corroded by the abuses of quarreling, jealousy, and violence. We are preoccupied with defending our turf, our rights, our privileges, our position, and our power. Even in places of worship, our petty histories of family struggle for positions of leadership deliver us to the grip of works of lightlessness.

Wake us up, Holy One, to what hour it is. Stir us out of our perpetual sleep. Awaken us to the reality that your day is at hand. Deliver us from the works of the night and cleanse us for the good works of the day.

We pray for the peace of the city, for the sake of our children, our companions, and our neighbors. We pray for peace on our streets and security within our homes. We call on your name in our churches. For the sake of your holy name and the healing of your household of faith, O sovereign God, bring peace within the sanctuary.

Bring us to a teachable attitude in this season of anticipation. Teach us in your way and equip us to walk in your path. Free us from our fears of others and the scary night, so that we may beat our assault weapons into plowshares and our handguns into belt buckles. Deliver all nations from the drive to use might to make right. Instill in our leaders a greater capacity to work for structures of peace. May war be a memory of the past. May peace be the wonder of tomorrow.   *Amen.*

Second Sunday of Advent

ISAIAH 11:1–10   ROMANS 15:4–13
PSALM 72:1–7, 18–19   MATTHEW 3:1–12

God of steadfast love, you come with an encouraging word in our baptism. You wade with us in the water and uphold us with renewing words of forgiveness. Even when we are not worthy of your grace, you come among us with your spirit to cleanse our wounded souls. Sin sick, we search for your word of assurance. We welcome it as you have welcomed us in Christ.

There are wild cries in the night, O God. There are voices of abused children crying in the wilderness of our cities. Their food is gleaned from the debris of despair. Their shelter is borrowed from the wreckage of squandered wealth. We hear you say to us, "You brood of vipers. Who warned you to flee from the wrath to come? Bear fruit that befits repentance, and do not presume to say to yourselves, 'We are good, tax-paying citizens with privilege, as were our fathers and mothers.'"

Compassionate God, wash us with the showers that water the earth. Deliver us from the dominion of presumed privilege. Redeem our lives so that we might joyously become helpers of the poor, healers of the weary, and homemakers of the needy. Move us by a spirit of wisdom and understanding that our desire to minister in your name may be a moment of peace in a hurting world.

With anticipation we await your coming. In good confidence we expect your spirit of knowledge and wisdom. Strengthen our faithfulness so that our desire and enthusiasm will bear fruit worthy of baptism.   *Amen.*

Third Sunday of Advent

ISAIAH 2:1–5   ROMANS 13:11–14
PSALM 122   MATTHEW 24:36–44

Holy God, whose mercy is from generation to generation, our spirits rejoice in who you are and in all you have done for us. You have drawn us close and favored us with the joy of living. In the desert of our souls, you plant a garden that blossoms when we are attuned to your Spirit. Your glory and majesty are far beyond our knowing, yet the glimpses we allow ourselves to receive strengthen our weak hands, firm our feeble knees, and lift our fearful hearts. You open our eyes and unstop our ears. We leap like deer, and our tongues sing for joy.

How seldom we allow ourselves such freedom and gladness. Instead, we aspire to becoming rich in things. We climb onto thrones of corporate achievement. We bang impatiently on the doors of material success. We are greedy for power and recognition, and so we grumble against one another and build walls to shut others out. We grow soft and comfortable inside our royal palaces while others are hungry, and we wonder why our hearts are not satisfied. O God, forgive us, and turn us around to follow your holy way.

On your highway, O God, we see the larger view of life. We can hear the prophets. We take note of your messengers. We know your judgments. Yet we also hear and believe good news. We realize that you have an important mission for us and that you equip us to accomplish the tasks you set before us. Strengthen our hearts that our spirits may rejoice in Christ our Savior.   *Amen.*

Fourth Sunday of Advent

ISAIAH 7:10–16   ROMANS 1:1–7
PSALM 80:1–7, 17–19   MATTHEW 1:18–25

Like Joseph, we have dreams, Creator God, but we attribute their meaning to a bad day at the office. Your call to vocation doesn't have a chance with us if it comes in a dream or a vision at the birthing of a new day. The promise of a new tomorrow in the birth of a child we haven't conceived? It's a nightmare, O God. Say it isn't so.

Where is our angel, O Holy Spirit? In the gift of a child called Immanuel! Oh no. Say it isn't so, mighty spirit. Our tomorrow in the hands of an anticipated birth of a present child? You have got to be kidding, God! A child doesn't have a chance to get a hearing in our world. Oh, so that's the way it's going to be? The gospel concerning the child of God, a relative of old King David, according to the flesh, is it? Well, God, you are stretching our hearts and minds if you expect us to accept this one.

Forgive our dullness of mind and spirit that we cannot willingly accept a simple sign of your mystery and majesty, amazing God. We pray for brighter days, but we world-weary mortals have lost confidence in our child. Free us in this season of your Advent to notice your appearance in the amazing wonder and excitement of a child concerning a new day dawning. Help us to accept a childlike freedom to choose the good news in the gift of another tomorrow.

Restore us, O God. Let your face shine through the joyous smile of a child. Come to heal our eyes and hearts hardened by the burden of tears. Give us the gift of new life, and restore unto us a vision of your coming to save. Give ear, O Shepherd, to the people of faith, and hear our prayer.   *Amen.*

Reflections

The Christmas Season

Reflections

Christmas Eve/Day, Proper 1 (A, B, C)

ISAIAH 9:2–7
PSALM 96

TITUS 2:11–14
LUKE 2:1–14, (15–20)

Your grace has appeared, O God, and we are full of song. How great you are, and greatly to be praised. We tremble before you, yet our hearts are glad. You have brought beauty and strength among us. Your light has penetrated our gloom. Let the heavens be glad. Let the earth rejoice.

Yet, the people of this earth are not moved for long. The unjust decrees continue. The oppression goes on and on, through the years. The light which we glimpse in our times of worship too often goes out as we make our decisions in the world. We make no room in the inn for those we label undeserving. We are afraid of people who are not like us. We are terrified when our advantages are threatened. How can a child be a sign for us? How can a helpless infant change our hearts?

And yet it happens. You touch our lives unexpectedly. We gather out of custom and find ourselves moved in unaccustomed ways. Your judgments are suddenly real, and yet somehow not threatening. Your truth flows through our worldly passions and makes us aspire to godly living. Our hopes are awakened, and our zeal is inspired. We want to sing with the angels, "Glory to God in the highest heaven, and on earth peace among all the people."

Gracious and loving God, show us how to live in peace. Become the center of each and every human life. Become the reference point for our daily choices. Equip us for self-controlled, upright, and godly living, in the name of One who has come among us as Wonderful Counselor, Mighty God, Everlasting Guide, Author of Peace.   *Amen.*

Christmas Day, Proper 2 (A, B, C)

ISAIAH 62:6–12   TITUS 3:4–7
PSALM 97   LUKE 2:(1–7), 8–20

Gracious God, the universe you made is your home. A tiny orb spinning in
your space is our earth home. We thank you for this gift called home. For you,
O God, are over all the earth. You are exalted far above all gods. We rejoice in
the wonders your heavens proclaim and give thanks to you, O Holy One.

Homemaking God, many in your family have no home to call their own.
Each day your children wander through the city looking for shelter. But shelter
is not home. Forgive us, Holy One, that our thoughts of going home for the
holiday blot out the pain of the homeless. Enable us to make room in our minds
and in our holiday giving for building houses for those who have no place to call
home. May a vision of your goodness and loving kindness, O God, our Savior,
move us to a renewal of spirit. Enlist us as prophets who will never be silent,
who will take no rest until homes are erected for all your children.

Go with us, Creator of Mary and Joseph, as we enlist ourselves in the
journey of faith. We pledge ourselves to the truth, found in the birthing of the
Word made flesh. May those who gather in the inns of the world this day hear
heavenly hosts proclaim:

> Glory to God in the Highest,
>
> and on earth peace among those
>
> with whom God is pleased.   *Amen.*

Christmas Day, Proper 3 (A, B, C)

ISAIAH 52:7–10
PSALM 98

HEBREWS 1:1–4, (5–12)
JOHN 10:1–14

Astonishing God, you listen as a sentinel to the speech of your creation. Much of it is banal and gross, and it flows as a torrent in the gutters of our cities and countryside. You listen caringly, amazing God, for a word of praise to interrupt the profanity of our mean media messages.

Forgive us, O Shepherd, for our easy acceptance and use of speech which robs you of praise and steals from us our self-respect. Grant us the grace to cultivate once more the speech of a gracious and generous life. Help us to hear your life-giving word: "I come that you may have life and have it abundantly. I am the good shepherd. The good shepherd is willing to die for the sheep. I am the good shepherd. I know my own, and my own know me, just as God the parent knows me and I know God. I freely lay down my life for you." Help us to receive and to believe the trustworthy Word you freely share with us, living Christ.

The strong arm of your Word, O God, is hoped for by your people. May the fear of your power, O God, be a restraining force to the oppressive means used by tyrants and self-serving leaders. May all those who abuse their power, mighty God, be rolled up like a coat and become a footstool for your feet. Free us, Sovereign One, to serve you for the sake of those who hope to inherit salvation.   *Amen.*

First Sunday after Christmas Day

ISAIAH 63:7–9   HEBREWS 2:10–18
PSALM 148   MATTHEW 2:13–23

Praise God, all people of faith. Praise God in highest heaven. Praise God, all the earth. We are gathered to sing your praises, glorious God, to marvel at the sun and moon and stars, to wonder at mountains and valleys, birds and animals, sunshine and snowy days. Most of all, your revelation in Jesus Christ draws us together in amazement at the way of love that claims us as brothers and sisters.

We confess that we have not lived as your children. We have dealt falsely with one another. We have lashed out against those who differ from us or who seem to stand in our way. Our fears have enslaved us. Our greed has blinded us to the consequences of our deeds. O God, we do not want to continue as competitors. We want to realize among us the oneness proclaimed in Christ's atoning sacrifice for our sins. Release us, O God, from the powers of death so that we may truly live.

Thank you, God, for rescuing us from the clutches of anxiety and cowardice. You are teaching us that the plots and tricks of humanity's evil ways do not have the last word. The fury of enemies cannot prevail. We are grateful for your steadfast love that ever seeks our best. When times of testing come, you are present to help us.

We pray for all who need your special direction and support today. Lead and guide those whose decisions shape the relationships between nations and the well-being of citizens. Alert us to ways that our participation in church and community can be an influence for good.   *Amen.*

Holy Name of Jesus (A, B, C)

January 1

NUMBERS 6:22–27
PSALM 8

GALATIANS 4:4–7 OR PHILIPPIANS 2:5–11
LUKE 2:15–21

We take your name, O Jesus, in our baptism. Your holy name marks our heads and our bodies as signs of your purpose in the world. Your name, Jesus, was a gift of God to you and to us. It was whispered to many by an angel, and it was announced to the world by a Roman ruler.

Help us to keep pondering in our hearts the mystery of your name's meaning for our lives. You desire that our lives be transformed by the power and presence of your name. Empower us each day to selflessly perform random acts of kindness that proclaim the goodness of your presence.

The majesty of your name, Jesus Christ, echoes through the heavens and the earth. Young children sing "Jesus loves me" with gusto and joy. Fearful and troubled, we move cautiously into the day singing your name: "Take the name of Jesus with you, child of sorrow and of woe." O God, our sovereign, how majestic is your name in all the earth.

Move us beyond our timid faith, O God, so that we can be unpretentious bearers of your name. Equip us to be generous human beings mindful of you and the needs of all neighbors. May simple acts of hospitality be the means by which we bless our family, work, and world in your name. Come, Christ Jesus, be our guest. Permit us to be your blessing in the world. In your holy name, we pray.

Amen.

New Year's Day (A, B, C)

January 1

ECCLESIASTES 3:1–13   REVELATIONS 21:1–6a
PSALM 8   MATTHEW 25:31–46

The horn of your salvation blows this night, holy God. Who will hear it and receive it? We tip our party hats to you as we roar off to celebrate the gift of a new year. Grant to us, generous God, the simple capacity to see the precious gift of your new day. You have given the gift of a new person, Jesus Christ, our redeemer.

You come in your glory, Savior of all, to call our attention to the thirsty ones. You help us to notice not only that impure water brings disease, but also that the lack of cool, clean water brings death. In another's thirst, Holy One, you want us to hear your words: "I thirst." A cup of cold water in your name, thirsty One, we will generously give.

You come, O Naked One, knowing what it is to have your cloak torn off and be exposed to the world. You beckon us to notice, as we run to the party, that many people are covered with tattered rags. Naked in the bitter cold of winter, Gracious One, we need eyes to see and a generous spirit to give a garment, to change rags into a rich covering which expresses your caring.

God, in the silent hours of this new year, we look for a new heaven and a new earth. We long to see a new city fashioned not by the cunning of human kind. No, we long for a city whose builder and maker is the Holy One. We call to you for a safe city where you dwell with us. We pray for a city where violent death does not frequently come, where mourning and crying and pain will be no more. In your new year, O God, come and transform us so that we can in a renewed spirit participate in renewing the places where we live.   *Amen.*

Second Sunday After Christmas Day (A, B, C)

JEREMIAH 31:7–14 OR SIRACH 24:1–12   EPHESIANS 1:3–14
PSALM 147:12–20 OR WISDOM OF SOLOMON 10:15–21   JOHN 1:(1–9), 10–18

Eternal God, whose Word was spoken in the creation of the universe, and in human words through men and women of many cultures and languages, we thank you for the Word made flesh in Jesus Christ. We marvel at the light Jesus brought among us, granting insight, healing broken lives, inspiring hope. Far beyond the guidance and constraints of the law, Jesus brought us your grace and love and pointed us to you, the source of life.

We confess that we have not always believed. Like the people of Nazareth, we have been skeptical, not accepting. We hesitate to trust the idea of incarnation or to let ourselves know and be known by Jesus Christ. How can we live with such grace and truth? How can we dare to embrace the true light when there is so much despair in the world, and in our own souls?

Yet you continue to pour out spiritual blessings. You assure us that we are chosen, accepted, and beloved. You adopt us as your own children, to walk in holiness, blameless before you. You redeem us, forgive us, and reveal to us the mystery of who you are and who you intend for us to be. The gospel of salvation fills us with hope. The promise of the Holy Spirit suffuses us with joy and praise. How wonderful are all your works, O God.

Save all your people, we pray. Bring them together from the farthest parts of the earth. Take away the faults and limitations, the sadness and weeping, the tears and anger, the violence and distress. Lead the nations on the paths of peace, bring comfort and joy, radiance and goodness, into the lives of all earth's people. We pray in Jesus' name. *Amen.*

Reflections

Reflections

Epiphany and the
Season Following

Reflections

Epiphany of Jesus (A, B, C)

ISAIAH 60:1–6
PSALM 72:1–7, 10–14

EPHESIANS 3:1–12
MATTHEW 2:1–12

Through the mystery of your mercy, Sovereign One, you have called us to be servants of the gospel of Jesus Christ. We marvel that you have moved us to be caretakers of the gift of the gospel. Many times we too, like Paul, feel that we are the very least of all the saints. Yet you quietly encourage us to be stewards of the mystery of your light in the world.

You said, "Let there be light," and the earth began to blossom with all forms of life. You named Jesus "Light of the World," and our lives came to birth and life in wondrous ways. Your light, precious God, takes our hands, leads us on, lets us stand for the Word made flesh. There are days when your eternal purpose for this time and this world are not clear to us. It is clouded by anxiety of profession and family, finance and education, moving and staying, and pain and suffering. We are fixed on these and forgetful that we have access to you in boldness and confidence through faith in Jesus, the Light of the World.

Help us to fall on our knees like the Magi. Their knowledge of the mystery of the universe, of mathematics, of geography, of Eastern religions did not blind them to the mystery made known to them in the face of a child. In that face, they saw your wisdom shining as a light to guide them in their search for truth. In the face of Jesus, they saw a bright morning star who would bless their day with a mystery of hope. In the glowing face of Jesus, they perceived a love which was gracious enough to be the redeemer of humankind. Come, Light of the World, and in your light may we see eternal life.   *Amen.*

Baptism of Jesus

ISAIAH 42:1–9
PSALM 29

ACTS 10:34–43
MATTHEW 3:13–17

God of strength and glory, we worship you in all your holy splendor. Your voice thunders over the waters. It flashes fire and shakes the foundations of the earth. Your voice calls us together in awe and wonder to praise your mighty deeds and seek your divine intent.

When we pause to contemplate who you are, our hearts sink, aware that we have not honored you with our lives. We have fashioned idols that consume our time and devotion. We confuse wants with needs and so spend our efforts accumulating things. We make choices according to our immediate gratification, not according to the greater good. We discriminate against people who are different from us. We ignore your calls for justice. We forget the meaning of our baptism and the promises we have made as a covenant people. Ever-present God, we beg your forgiveness.

We are confident of your pardon and the transforming power of your spirit. You take our bruised and fainting psyches, crushed by disappointments, and lift us up to new life. You give breath to your people, opening the eyes of the blind, releasing us from the prisons we make for ourselves and others. You turn our good intentions to good deeds. Your healing power recreates the church, calling forth our faithful witness. Praise be to you, O God.

May we see all people as your beloved children. Grant us courage to reach out to them with forgiving love when we feel wronged. Give us tongues to share the good news of the gospel, testifying to what we have seen and heard. May we live what we preach so others will be drawn into the service of Jesus Christ. Anoint us with your Holy Spirit and with power.   *Amen.*

Second Sunday after the Epiphany

ISAIAH 49:1–7

PSALM 40:1–11

I CORINTHIANS 1:1–9

JOHN 1:29–42

Redeemer of all nations, you have given us a calling from the womb of a community of faith. You have equipped us with speech like a two-edged sword. Through calling and equipping us, O Savior of nations, you expect us to evoke the spirit of your servant, Jesus Christ.

We thank you for the gift of Christ's abiding presence. The certainty of your nearness brings glad news of sure deliverance in the great congregation. By the energy of your voice, we form a new song in our mouths. It sings of blessing for those who put their trust in God. It soars with the music of wondrous deeds and thoughts of your compassion toward all human beings. Gratitude is in our hearts for your saving help and steadfast love.

God of all faithfulness and all comfort, your congregation is troubled by timidness of spirit and faintness of heart. Its eyes are fixed on the glory of past days and blind to the testimony of Christ confirmed among it. It recalls the wonders of former years and cannot see the quiet miracle of new persons who enter its fellowship. You are faithful to us, gracious God, through joyous light seen in the faces of new and old friends who affirm the grace of our Savior, Jesus Christ. The love of God and the joyous fellowship of the Holy Spirit is with every one of us.

Amen.

Third Sunday after the Epiphany

ISAIAH 9:1–4   I CORINTHIANS 1:10–18
PSALM 27:1, 4–9   MATTHEW 4:12–23

From the deep shadows that surround us, we come to your light, O God of
our salvation. You are the stronghold of our lives. In you, we rejoice and find
our true home. When we know ourselves to be in your presence, our fears are
overcome. We are no longer afraid of enemies, real or imagined.

We rejoice before you today, for our burdens are being lifted, and the yoke
of oppression is broken. You free us to see your beauty and to inquire in your
temple. You liberate our spirits to appreciate the value of our own lives and to
treasure those with whom we share this brief existence on earth.

We confess that other people are often a puzzle to us. We do not
understand their ways or appreciate what they do. Their loyalties differ from
ours. Even in the church, we see things from many different points of view. We
are divided over matters that are less important than we make them. How we
were baptized and by whom becomes more significant to us than the meaning of
our baptism. The message of the cross becomes mere foolishness to us as we
forget the saving power it represents. Through our divisions, we yet hear your
call to repentance. Forgive us, we pray.

In the presence of your forgiving love, we also hear Christ's compelling call
to discipleship. Grant us the courage to follow, to leave behind the distractions
and lesser loyalties, to make central working for your reign among us. We have
good news to share that is healing and life-giving. Unite us in this central
imperative to serve in Christ's name.   *Amen.*

Fourth Sunday after the Epiphany

MICAH 6:1–8   I CORINTHIANS 1:18–31

PSALM 15   MATTHEW 5:1–12

Holy God, help us to consider our call. We are tempted to see it in places of power, but not many of us are powerful. We are teased to consider it as connected with high society, but not many of us are of noble birth. We are titillated by thoughts that it is discovered in the places of the mighty, but few of us are from the households of strength. Many of us are convinced it is revealed in the subtle havens of human wisdom, but most of us are not wizards of intellectual work.

O wise God, our Savior, deliver us from the cleverness of the clever. Open our minds and hearts to the strength of our call in Christ Jesus, whom God made our wisdom, our strength, and our redemption.

Holy One, you are the strong foundation of the earth. It is you who call your people to speak words from the heart. It is you who whisper in our minds to stand firm for justice in our community. It is you who demand that we have mercy above the desire for revenge. It is you, O God, who tenderly encourage us to walk humbly with you through places where people suffer for righteousness' sake. Equip us to walk in the pathway of peace, Prince of Peace, that we may truly see the faces of the children of God. Enable us to shed the tears of the strong, that we may passionately know the comfort of those who mourn. Assist us as we try each day to sojourn with you as servants of the Compassionate One, who enfold to their hearts neighbors in need. Then quicken our ears to hear, "Come dwell with me on my holy hill." Be at peace. *Amen.*

Fifth Sunday after the Epiphany

ISAIAH 58:1–9a, (9b–12)
PSALM 112:1–9, (10)

I CORINTHIANS 2:1–12, (13–16)
MATTHEW 5:13–20

Powerful God, we draw near with fasting and humility. We want to know your ways and live in your righteousness. Surely you will hear us and favor us. You promise riches to those who fear you and delight in your commandments. Here we are, ready to represent the mind of Christ, to teach your wisdom and bring others to your truth. We will shine as lights and give you the glory.

We say those brave words, and then we hear a quiet voice deep within that questions our sincerity and faithfulness. We have rebelled against you, feeling that life has not been fair. We are more focused on our own interests than on your service. Pursuit of our own advantages leads to the oppression of others. When we feed the hungry, we do not risk our own bread. While we minister to the homeless, we are reluctant to open our own doors to them. Sometimes the hardest people to get along with are our own next of kin. Help us and heal us, O God, and let your light shine into our lives.

Thank you for renewing the best you have placed within us. Steady our hearts that we will not be afraid to demonstrate your love for all people. Send your spirit among us to strengthen our faith and fill us with a wisdom far greater than our own conclusions. Equip us to be salt and light. Shine through us that your rule may prevail in the church and wherever we scatter to serve. May our humility be genuine and our service truly selfless. May all we do honor Christ and give you the glory. *Amen.*

Sixth Sunday after the Epiphany

DEUTERONOMY 30:15–20

PSALM 119:1–8

I CORINTHIANS 3:1–9

MATTHEW 5:21–37

Generous God, you pour out the wealth of your goodness, and the world blooms with abundant plants in glorious color. Refreshing rains restore the earth and an abundant array of living things splash and wade in the water of life. Thank God for our Creator's goodness.

Forgiving God, look in mercy on your ministering ones who stumble and fall face-first into the murky waters of self-importance. Many of us call attention to our planting ("my church"), to our watering ("I baptized"), and to our cultivating ("I took in so many"). You do not address us as a spiritual people, Holy One, for you clearly see us indulging ourselves in competitive ways. Call us to a renewed vision of God's coworkers, in God's world and in God's congregation. Thank you, God, for the joy and freedom of your forgiveness.

Liberating God, your presence and your purpose is focused on freeing all who carry unjust burdens. Free us from a piety which is blind to the bitter hardships of poverty. Quicken our thought and passion to the consequence of denied freedom, neglected justice, abused children, violence in the street, decaying neighborhoods, broken families, lost jobs, and nations making war.

We call for blood, O God. We vote for old solutions. Amen for "an eye for an eye and a tooth for a tooth." "It's in the book," we cry. It's our old piety at work. We fail to hear Christ's Word: "But I say to you, give to the one who begs from you. Love your enemies and pray for those who persecute you so that you may be children of God, for God makes the sun rise on the evil and on the good and sends rain on the just and on the unjust." Thank you, healing Christ, for your liberating Word which calls us back from the brink of self-destruction to the high ground of being drum majors for justice.   *Amen.*

Seventh Sunday after the Epiphany

LEVITICUS 19:1–2, 9–18
PSALM 119:33–40

I CORINTHIANS 3:10–11, 16–23
MATTHEW 5:38–48

Holy God, you send your Spirit to dwell in us. How amazing is your love for us. You make the sun to rise on the evil and on the good. You send rain on the righteous and the unrighteous alike. We reap the harvest of your lands and enjoy the bounty you provide. Your grace has come to us in Jesus Christ. How great are your ways, O God.

We confess that we have profaned your name, both by our actions and by our neglect. We have stripped our lands of their wealth and left little for others. Our lies multiply as we look out for ourselves in ways that are costly to our neighbors. We often fail to include those with disabilities in our planning and our programs. We delight in excluding people we label as enemies and are quick to retaliate against those who offend us. O God, we do not want to slander or bear grudges. We are repelled by human hatred and the shedding of blood. Deliver us from the shadow side of ourselves. Let your forgiving love forever change the way we relate to one another.

Thank you for your message to the congregation: "You shall be holy." Thank you for teaching us the way of your statutes and leading us in the path of your commandments. You have made us your temple and are eager to dwell within us. We have only to acknowledge your presence.

Help us to embrace your wisdom instead of the world's foolishness. We want to build this church, and our individual lives, on the foundation of Jesus Christ. May we learn to pray for those with whom we disagree and grow into that perfect love which you pour out on us.   *Amen.*

Eighth Sunday after the Epiphany

ISAIAH 49:8–16a

PSALM 131

I CORINTHIANS 4:1–5

MATTHEW 6:24–34

Sing, O heavens, and be joyful, O earth. Break forth in singing, O mountains, for God comforts all people. Thank you, joyful God, for the light which brings life to all who suffer afflictions from human history.

May the parents of hungry children see the morning when food will be daily bread. May communities with dry wells see a daybreak when pumps will pour forth to fill every cup with cool, clear water. May the homeless see a sunrise which will call them not back to the streets but to a place of purpose and dignity. May the wounded spirit experience a wake-up call which places the Balm of Gilead on the sin-sick soul.

Bring your steadfast love, O God, your salvation according to your promise. May the light of your mercy dawn on the judgmental minds and hearts of many who think they believe. Heal us all of our hair-trigger quickness to judge others by standards we ourselves fail to meet. Deliver us from the court of this human heart. There confusion reigns, and its judgments bring suffering to all. By your mercy, dear God, forgive.

May the light of all those who love you, O God, shine in the face of Jesus Christ upon all the anxious hearts. Let their anxiety about life find healing in your gracious Word. Let the day's own trouble be sufficient for the day. Do not, therefore, be anxious about tomorrow, for tomorrow will be anxious for itself. Thank you, God, for the gift of your abiding presence.   *Amen.*

Ninth Sunday after the Epiphany

DEUTERONOMY 11:18–21, 26–28   ROMANS 1:16–17, 3:22b–28, (29–31)
PSALM 31:1–5, 19–24   MATTHEW 7:21–29

Creator God, your light is brighter than a thousand suns. In this light, you peer through the veil of our fearful nights to illumine eyes crusted with grief. You see our strength failing because of distress. You notice our souls and our bodies sighing for relief.

Gracious God, deliver us and rescue us speedily. Listen carefully to our prayers, and take heed to the spirit of our petitions. Fill us with courage to be faithful to the Word we hear. The winds of troubled lives blow against the frail fabric of the household of faith. Many wait to hear the Word but lack the spirit to live it out. Others hang words in their homes, wear your sign around their necks, and tape bumper stickers before our eyes, yet they fail to diligently keep the spirit and the letter of your Word. Our lives are like houses built upon the sand. The storms of life beat upon us, and we are in danger of collapsing. Lift us up on your rock of refuge. Lead us and guide us for your name's sake.

Your gospel, O Holy One, holds the power of salvation for everyone who has faith. Inspire us to live beyond our distress and fears in the gospel revealed through faith for faith. Open our eyes to see your embracing presence, and help us to accept that "whoever through faith is righteous will live." Empower us, Creator God, to receive your blessing. Let your face shine on your children. Save us in your steadfast love.   *Amen.*

Last Sunday after the Epiphany (Transfiguration Sunday)

EXODUS 34:12–18

PSALM 2 OR PSALM 99

2 PETER 1:16–21

MATTHEW 17:1–9

God of the mountaintop and of the valley, we look up to view your majesty. We listen with fear and trembling for your Word. We are filled with awe as your glory surrounds us. Touch us by your Holy Spirit that we may feel your presence with us in this hour.

We confess our discomfort with words of warning, talk of devouring fire and voices from heaven. We are impatient when we are asked to watch and wait. When we have a complaint or a request, we want action, and we want it now. How could Moses spend forty days and forty nights attending to your Word and waiting for your instructions? We are more likely to join the plotters down in the valley. In our busy lives, we want solutions, not long silences and deferred answers to our hurried prayers.

Still, we long for meanings that elude us. We are not happy with our frantic pace that so easily becomes dull routine. There are days when we doubt our own value and worth. We're not sure that our insights and interpretations have any merit. Let your truth dawn on us, we pray, like a lamp shining into lightless places. Send your morning star to rise in our hearts and bring your new day into our midst.

As we journey with the disciples to the Mount of Transfiguration, we hear again your affirmation of Jesus, and know that it is also meant for us. Jesus said to the disciples, "Do not be afraid," and you also summon us to get up and venture without fear into another week. Thank you for loving us and raising us to new life.

Amen.

Reflections

Reflections

The Lenten Season

Reflections

Ash Wednesday (A, B, C)

JOEL 2:1–2, 12–17 OR ISAIAH 58:1–12   2 CORINTHIANS 5:20b–6:10
PSALM 51:1–17   MATTHEW 6:1–6, 16–21

"Have mercy on us, O God, according to your steadfast love; according to your abundant mercy blot out our transgressions." We daily live beyond the boundaries of gracious living, Holy God. The facts of life are twisted to enhance appearances of righteousness. The truth claims of our speech are deceiving so that reputations can be enlarged. The honor of relationships with neighbors is harmed in order that we might win a game, a job, or an election.

Purge us of deceptive living that we can come clean. Scrub us, and we shall be pure as snow. Hide not your face from our sins, and cause us to remember all our deceptive practices. Deliver us from the self-serving habit of blaming others for our sins. Bring us to the joy of your salvation, and lift us up to a way of living which is pleasing in your sight.

Gracious God, as we enter the hidden places of our memory and the quiet corners of our hearts, open to us the grace of sins forgiven. May the mystery of your mercy strengthen our capacity to honor the gift of spiritual discipline. Equip us to embrace the heavenly treasures of kindness and transparent character. Open our hearts and minds to see clearly the genuine need of our neighbor. Mold us in purity of heart to will one thing—namely, to love you with all our mind and strength and to love our neighbors as ourselves. Receive our prayer in Jesus Christ's name. *Amen.*

First Sunday in Lent

GENESIS 2:15–17; 3:1–7
PSALM 32

ROMANS 5:12–19
MATTHEW 4:1–11

As this season of reflection and preparation begins, we turn to you, O Creator, seeking direction for our journey through the disappointments and trials of life. You are a hiding place for us in times of trouble. Your steadfast love surrounds us amid the storms and distresses we face. Your Word is a guide to us, and your counsel instructs us in the way we should go.

We confess our transgressions before you. We have eaten of forbidden fruit and caused others to do the same. We give in to the temptations of our materialistic surroundings. The kingdoms of this world beckon us with their charms. We delight in the prospect of success and fame and power. We like to play God in the little realms where we fancy ourselves in control. We become like mules, without understanding, whose tempers must be curbed and whose stubbornness shuts out the guidance you long to give us. Forgive us, we pray.

We are happy when our transgressions are forgiven. When we turn from deceit and acknowledge our sin, you lift us up. We feel like shouting for joy when we are freed from the burden of our doubts and disobedience. We cannot live by bread alone—we know that. We are in no position to put you to the test. We recognize the limitations of our humanity. There is no God but you, and we are called to serve you. That is good news, not a burden.

Hear our prayers for all who suffer, for all who are troubled and afraid, for all who dwell in the shadows and reject the light, for all who suffer the torments of the wicked, for all who dwell in the death of sin. Help us to be carriers of your redeeming, reconciling grace. *Amen.*

Second Sunday in Lent

GENESIS 12:1–4a   ROMANS 4:1–5, 13–17
PSALM 121   JOHN 3:1–17 OR MATTHEW 17:1–9

We lift up our eyes to the hills, O God, seeking the help that comes only from you. You have blessed us again and again, far beyond our deserving. You help us in so many ways that we do not pause to recognize. Day after day, you go with us, keeping us from evil and preserving in us the gift of life.

O God, we are sorry for the many times we fail to express our gratitude or acknowledge our indebtedness to you. We grab for the world's goods as our rightful inheritance, forgetting the claims of your other children. We are more ready to argue the fine points of the law than we are to obey. We engage in endless debate rather than surrender ourselves to the leading of your spirit. Save us, we pray, from the evil we so often tolerate and perpetuate.

Thank you for loving the world so much that you sent Jesus to save us from ourselves and introduce us to eternal life. In Christ we are reborn, and each day becomes a glorious gift of new beginnings. Thank you for cleansing waters and your renewing Spirit. Thank you for the revelation of heavenly things. You fill our earthly existence with vast possibilities as you bless the families of this earth. By your grace, we can become a great church, a great nation, a peaceful world.

Bless all who come to you, whether under cover of night or in the light of day. Send the winds of your Spirit to astonish and transform the hurting world. Help us to believe and to live by faith. We would offer your saving love to the world in all we say and do.   *Amen.*

Third Sunday in Lent

EXODUS 17:1–7   ROMANS 5:1–11
PSALM 95   JOHN 4:5–42

Merciful God, you recall all the generations of humankind with sadness. Tears of pain have washed your face as you watch the bloodletting on this earth. We are a people whose hearts have strayed down the path of violence. Our media glorifies it to sell products, and our homes sow seeds for it with passive acceptance. Each night we hid behind locked doors in fear of murder, and then we watch the madness of murder on TV.

We are a people whose hearts have gone astray. We have guns; they are our savior. The bullet is our might. It will rescue us from the unknown threat of night. We boast in the false courage our weapons appear to give. And in the night a child blows the brains out of another child because of a handgun that was meant to save us.

Merciful God, we are a people whose minds have gone astray. Who will relieve us from this household of death? Help us to drink the water of a living savior, Jesus Christ. May the peace of Christ so wash our minds, our hearts, our souls, and our hands that we might surrender our obsession with oppressing power. Grant us the blessing of your mercy, that our minds can be open to positive ways of conquering our fears. By faith free us to come and see the anointed One who knows all we have done and yet loves us in truth. May the wonder of Christ's knowing and loving set us free to live a life of peace and grace.   *Amen.*

Fourth Sunday in Lent

I SAMUEL 16:1–13

PSALM 23

EPHESIANS 5:8–14

JOHN 9:1–41

We come to you, glorious God, for your light reveals the gloom in which we have lived. We did not know that we were blind until you taught us to see. There is so much more to life than we have allowed ourselves to experience. You open our eyes to the vast possibilities for helping others, overcoming injustice, and building community.

We have hesitated to enlist in your service. Our times teach us a different standard. We worship flashy success. We judge by appearances and seek the company of those who are attractive and powerful. We wrap ourselves in busyness lest we be bored by inactivity. We look for people to blame when things go wrong. We are skeptical of ideas and individuals whose patterns do not fit our own.

Amazing God, how patient you are to keep forgiving us, even when your light has shone into our lives and we persist in our blind spots. You invite us to lie down in green pastures beside still waters. When we allow ourselves to be quiet in your presence, we sense your goodness and mercy. In the midst of suffering and loss, we know an abiding peace as you comfort us. You fill our cups to overflowing. Dwelling in your love, we have no fear of enemies. Living in your light, we have nothing to hide.

Shepherd of all, reach out today to all who have not been gathered into your fold. Open the eyes of your struggling people to the signs of your loving providence that surround us on every hand. Quiet the scoffers and skeptics with evidence of your love. Let your astonishing good news be communicated through us to all we meet, and let the outreach of this church be a powerful witness to your life-giving truth.   *Amen.*

Fifth Sunday in Lent

EZEKIEL 37:1–14   ROMANS 8:6–11
PSALM 130   JOHN 11:1–45

Amazing God, out of the depths of the dry bones of life, we cry to you. Hear our prayer. Give careful attention to the yearnings of our hearts.

The fruits of setting our minds only on the flesh are producing a bitter harvest. Many people are dying because we love the easy benefits of the flesh. Merriment induced by booze and drugs ripens the mind for destructive violence. Indulgent abuse of the flesh destroys faithfulness to others and ourselves. Mindless kicks of the crowd or the gang for a joyride's sake brings sudden death to the flesh in the evening.

Agonizing God, we are surrounded by decaying flesh and bleached bones. Come near and heal our valleys, our cities of dry bones. You have great power to redeem a dying and decaying people. Take away the stone which covers the stench of our surrender to living only for this flesh. May the foul order of mean living arouse us from a mindless slumber at the edge of an urban grave.

God of life, may the life-giving power of Christ raise us up to a way of living that is renewing and refreshing. Revitalize your spirit within us, so that this mortal body can be motivated by the power of the Resurrected One, Jesus Christ, our Savior. Move us to believe that the living Christ can empower us to generate a new valley, a new city, and a new life from the dry bones of death. May we obey your redeeming call: "Come out! Live!"   *Amen.*

Sixth Sunday in Lent (Palm Sunday)

MATTHEW 21:1–11   PHILIPPIANS 2:5–11
PSALM 118:1–2, 19–29   MATTHEW 26:14–27:66 OR MATTHEW 27:11–54

Give thanks to God, persons of faith, for the gift of the Holy One, the child of God. Let each one of us empty ourselves of claims to fame and self-importance. Help us to throw aside our quest for grand positions of self-aggrandizement. Free us to renew your call to have the mind of Christ among ourselves. Deliver us of our propensity to claw, grab, push, and shove our way to the head of the pack and over the bodies of trampled brothers and sisters.

Pull us to the simple center of the mind of Christ. There, open our minds to the servant role of our Savior. Even though service for and with persons can be messy and unappreciated, help us to experience self-forgetfulness.

Gracious Jesus, you come to us in our daily encounters with persons in special need. They wait hopefully for one of your self-giving disciples. Your faithful ones see with open minds and hands those in need. You quietly call through the need of those who suffer. You wait to see if our profession of faith will lead to a simple deed of humble service. Servant Jesus, set our faces like flint on the person's need, on a people's suffering that compassionate care can follow. In responding, may we see the glory of God shining in the faces of those sighing with relief: "Thank God." People of faith see, believe, and care through simple acts of kindness. May all who believe that God can be trusted say   *Amen.*

Sixth Sunday in Lent (Passion Sunday)

ISAIAH 50:4–9a
PSALM 31:9–16

PHILIPPIANS 2:5–11
MATTHEW 26:14–27:66 OR MATTHEW 27:11–54

Living God, you come to us in the midst of death. Once again, our sins pave the way to the cross. Our desertion of others in their time of need separates us from Jesus. Our sleepy inattention means that some who are faithful must struggle alone. Our love of violence spreads seeds of destruction. Our distant discipleship and all-too-easy denial witness against the One who came to save us. We warm ourselves at the fires of greed, betraying innocent blood. We wash our hands of responsibility for the consequences of our sin. We demand proof of your reconciling presence in Jesus of Nazareth, even as we are dying in our own deceptions.

O God, empty us of all our petty schemes, our petulant scorn, our pious sinfulness. We are guilty of crimes against your love. We grieve the wasted opportunities that bring us to this time of judgment with no defense save the faithfulness of Jesus Christ. Stripped bare of all our pretense, we call on Christ to save us. Our trust is awakened. You are our God. Be gracious to us in our distress. You quiet our rebellion. You remove our disgrace. You lift us up from our shame and declare us "not guilty."

How amazing is your love for all your children. You awaken our generosity. You bring us good news. You empty the tombs that have been sealed and roll away the stones that separate us from life. Your face shines on your servants, and your steadfast love equips us for each day's tasks. Grant us the mind of Christ who did not count equality with you as something to be exploited. We would humble ourselves in obedience to your will. May your name be exalted in all the earth and every knee bend before Jesus, confessing our faith in word and deed. *Amen.*

Monday of Holy Week (A, B, C)

ISAIAH 42:1–9
PSALM 36:5–11

HEBREWS 9:11–15
JOHN 12:1–11

Life-giving God, your steadfast love extends to the heavens, and your faithfulness beyond the clouds. Your righteousness is higher than the mountains, and your judgments deeper than the sea. We take refuge in the shadow of your wings.

We have grown faint under the crushing burdens of life. There is so much injustice in the world, sometimes we feel like victims, bruised and battered by life. Sometimes we victimize and abuse others, often without knowing how our words wound or how our greed deprives others. Without your love, we dwell in shadows. Outside the covenant community, our lives are incomplete. By your redeeming grace in Jesus Christ, we are raised from death to new life, called to receive the promised inheritance of disciples.

Thank you, God, for accepting our dimly burning wicks and breathing us back to life as people aflame with your Spirit. You have kept us from breaking under the weight of sin and have lifted its burden from our shoulders. You have cared for us when we were lost and frightened. You have greeted our fumbling attempts at faithfulness with affirmation and encouragement. You turn our impulses to good ends and reframe our questionable actions into positive learnings. How precious is your steadfast love, O God.

We bring to you this day our concern for the world. The coastlands await your teaching. The poor cry out for bread. Those imprisoned in their own narrow concerns, who find no meaning in life, need the freedom only you can give. Establish justice in the earth, O God. Show us where our gifts are needed, and equip us to serve, in Jesus' name. *Amen.*

Tuesday of Holy Week (A, B, C)

ISAIAH 49:1–7   1 CORINTHIANS 1:18–31
PSALM 71:1–14   JOHN 12:20–36

Faithful One, you call us from the womb to enter your world as a serving community. You tease us to pay attention to helping activities which restore the survivors of tormenting deeds of our violent society.

Deliver us, O God, from the persistent temptation to hide behind closed doors in times of trouble. For our children's sake, rescue us from the grasp of cruel neglect of duty to be healing and reconciling presences in a fearful society.

O God, since our youth you have taught us the power of loving. Through the generous care of people in our homes, churches, schools, and communities, we have experienced the renewing energy of love. We have known that Jesus loved us through the self-giving generosity of friends, coaches, teachers, pastors, and neighbors. For the gift of your abiding presence, O God, in the caring of others, we give you thanks.

Faithful Savior, when your hour of trouble came, you did not run and hide behind closed doors. Even though your soul was troubled, you did not cower in fearful silence. With your face fixed on the divine presence, you prayed to be saved from the hour of trouble. We too pray to be saved from our temptation to surrender our cities, towns, and neighborhoods to the violence which grows from love denied and just claims ignored. Renew our trust in your gift of presence. Faithful God, equip us to persevere in the work of the cross. Come, faithful Savior, and redeem our time.   *Amen.*

Wednesday of Holy Week (A, B, C)

ISAIAH 50:4–9a   HEBREWS 12:1–3
PSALM 70   JOHN 13:21–32

Waken our ears, glorious God, to listen as those who are being taught the most important lessons of life. May we learn from the Pioneer and Perfector of our faith to love your salvation, to give ourselves without reserve, and to sustain the weary with a word. You alone can provide the courage we need to face insult, hostility, and shame with care, compassion, and firm resolve. May we not lose heart when our efforts seem in vain, when evil appears to prevail, and when even friends betray. O God, make haste to help your servants. Deliver us from our rebellions to stand with your Chosen One in these difficult days.

Like Peter, we have often been quick to speak, impulsive in our actions, and fearful when challenged. Like Judas, we have our own agendas and desire for personal gain. We are self-protective instead of pro-active. We find it hard to persevere in the face of difficulties. With the psalmist, we cry out that we are poor and needy. O God, deliver us, not for our sakes alone, but that we might be strengthened for the work you call us to do.

We lift up before you our violent, contentious world: those who are truly poor and needy, our sisters and brothers who have been neglected and abused, the victims of war, those who starve for bread, and all who are starved for love. The problems are so massive that we hardly know where to begin addressing them. The needs are so extensive that we are tempted to give up. Yet, surrounded by so great a cloud of witnesses, disciples, and apostles who have dared through the centuries to follow Jesus, we step forward today, saying: "Here we are. Send us."   *Amen.*

Holy Thursday (A, B, C)

EXODUS 12:1–4, (5–10), 11–14
PSALM 116:1–2, 12–19

I CORINTHIANS 11:23–26
JOHN 13:1–17, 31b–35

Almighty God, you pass through our communities and see blood pour out. You hear the sobbing of family and friends who mourn the death of a slaughtered child or youth. Precious in your sight, Holy One, are the lives of your children. Pass over our cities and deliver us from the daily burden of death.

Call us, strong deliverer, to pay all vows to you in the presence of all your people. In your house of prayer for all nations, may the sharing of a loaf of bread and the cup of salvation filled with wine be the moment when our eyes are opened to your embodied presence among us. Let our awareness that you are with us strengthen our resolve to overcome the snares of death which encompass our neighborhoods. Move us to call on your name that life may be saved.

Forgive us that we so easily surrender to the reality of unnecessary dying. We watch it on the television as if it were simply entertainment. Good God, deliver us from dullness of mind and coldness of heart. Free our souls from a matter-of-fact pleasure in watching human beings slaughtered for the entertainment of sick society. May our eyes fill with tears until we recover a land of the living.

Strengthen our faith, servant of God, that we might be freed to wash the feet of all who wander through the alleys of life. Grant us the grace to lift up the cup of salvation and call on your name. By your Spirit, may we respond as a serving people. May the servants of Christ say   *Amen.*

Good Friday (A, B, C)

ISAIAH 52:13–53:12   HEBREWS 10:16–25 OR HEBREWS 4:14–16; 5:7–9

PSALM 22   JOHN 18:1–19:42

We are face-to-face with human cruelty as we come to you in prayer, O God. The record of that Friday long ago is painful to read: the Great Teacher humiliated, despised, rejected; the Great Healer disfigured, bruised, and broken; the Great Caregiver deserted, unjustly charged, and cynically condemned. Alone in an unsympathetic crowd, the victim of a calculating plot and mass hysteria, Jesus carried love to the cross.

We find it hard to understand why this suffering was necessary. It doesn't make any sense. We are uncomfortably aware that we cannot simply condemn those who participated in the plot. When we point fingers at the religious leaders and then at the disciples, we know in our hearts that we would probably have acted no differently. We allow violence to continue in our own day. We tolerate the agony of innocent people. We do little to oppose the systems and practices that condemn others to the margins of society.

So we are in the garden with Judas, at the fire warming ourselves with Peter, at the judge's bench washing our hands with Pilate, and at Golgotha driving the nails. But perhaps a part of us is also at the foot of the cross, watching and waiting in quiet support. We are there to hear the last requests and receive our continuing commission. Perhaps we have been distant disciples, like Joseph of Arimathea, who are finally moved to action.

O God, show us a way out of Calvary, not that we may avoid its pain but that we might build on its witness. May some who have been bystanders become involved with Christ as new disciples and apostles. Help us consider how to provoke one another to love and good deeds and to give encouragement in Christ's name. *Amen.*

Holy Saturday (A, B, C)

JOB 14:1–14 OR LAMENTATIONS 3:1–9, 19–24   I PETER 4:1–8
PSALM 31:1–4, 15–16   MATTHEW 27:57–66 OR JOHN 19:38–42

Eternal God, we earnestly guard our days as we hurry from our tombs. We fear the unexpected and the unknown. We seek refuge in you, O God. Be a rock of support for us. For your name's sake, O Sovereign One, lead and guide us out of the tomb of despair into the light of Easter morning. Let your face shine on your servant people. Save us in your steadfast love.

Precious Savior, take us by the hand and lead us to the places where the saints rest from their labors. There, where marble markers honor their names, aid us to affirm our own mortality. Help us to honestly admit that each one of us is no better than you. You died. Your flesh experienced the lightlessness and the dampness of the tomb. Your spirit was grasped by the power of the grave. Your hope for eternal life was dimmed by the stone which sealed your resting place.

Thank you, gracious child of God, for your obedience to the purpose of God. With fear and trembling, and yet courage and faith, you took on our fear of the grave. Guide us in our reflection on your three days in the tomb. Keep us focused on our own mortality, so that we can appreciate the amazing gift of grace in the dawning of a new day. Aid our seeing that we can experience the resurrection opportunities of the day. May our days be driven not by impulses of human desire but by the purpose of God for the renewal of our lives.

Living Christ, raise us up to a level of living where we might dwell in the Spirit as God does.   *Amen.*

Reflections

The Easter Season

Reflections

Easter Vigil (A, B, C)

Eternal God, beyond all the boundaries of time and space, your love has created and continues to create energy and abundance. All of human history is a mere speck on the vast horizons of your creativity. The wonder of it all brings praise to our lips as we declare: "Your steadfast love endures forever." You have been a refuge and strength to the likes of Noah—people who trust you in the midst of adversity, who take the time to be still and know that you are God.

We wonder, O God, what you might require of us. Sometimes our hearing is faulty, and we almost make the wrong sacrifices. Our families suffer when time and devotion are invested elsewhere. Our faith needs correction, as did Abraham's. We bless you, O God, for the counsel you give us when we are open to it. Your presence is with us amid Egyptian oppression and stark days in the wilderness. When we are thirsty, you invite us to refreshing waters. You lift our thoughts above our earthbound existence, for your ways are not our ways. We listen for your wisdom. The heavens declare your glory and reveal your perfect law.

We confess our lack of attention, O God. Too often we seem content to dwell in the valley of dry bones, cut off from communion with you. We lose hope, and our spirits faint within us. There is no new song to sing. Yet we have been baptized into Christ Jesus, and you promise to unite us in resurrection. You call us out of our slavery to things, to experience a new dawning. You shake the foundations we have built and greet us with new life. O God, help us to see Jesus.   *Amen.*

Easter Day

ACTS 10:34–43 OR JEREMIAH 31:1–6   COLOSSIANS 3:1–4 OR ACTS 10:34–43
PSALM 118:1–2, 14–24   JOHN 20:1–18 OR MATTHEW 28:1–10

We hear the glad songs of victory, and we are amazed. We have heard the story of Easter many times, but after the anguish of Good Friday and the emptiness of Saturday, it still comes as a surprise—a bewildering surprise. With the women who loved Jesus, we feel the depths of grief and sorrow as they plan to minister to a dead body. We sense their bewilderment and fear when, instead, they encounter an empty tomb. O God, how can it be? The One on whom we depended has been taken from us, and now even the body is gone.

There are skeptics among us, O God, even to this day. We cannot see the One standing among us, offering us life. To set our minds on things of your realm means letting go of the things of this earth that have become so important to us. We weep more over these losses than over a broken relationship with Jesus. We confess that the gates of righteousness do not beckon us so much as the doors of a department store. We are anchored on earth among all we have built, and the chief cornerstone of life might still be in a grave, for all we know, most of the time.

Then Easter comes, and excitement breaks out in spite of us. We join our voices in the words of the psalmist: I shall not die, but I shall live, and recount the deeds of God. This is the day that you, O God, have made. We will rejoice and be glad in it. Your steadfast love endures forever. Then Jesus says, "Greetings," and calls our name. The good news becomes part of our story, a story we must share. Thank you, God. *Amen.*

Easter Day

Alternate

ACTS 10:34–43 OR JEREMIAH 31:1–6   COLOSSIANS 3:1–4 OR ACTS 10:34–43
PSALM 118:1–2, 14–24   JOHN 20:1–18 OR MATTHEW 28:1–10

Risen Savior, like Peter and John we do not know the scripture that you must rise from the dead. We too go back to our homes perplexed by the fact of an empty tomb. We sing, "Christ the Lord Is Risen Today!" Yet this inspiring proclamation seldom energizes our commitment to an Easter faith.

Your resurrection from the dead announces that God's promise of eternal life is made good. Our Creator's steadfast love endures forever. The grave, the tomb, and the death are not victory. God's steadfast love is the gift which endures forever. Forgive our blind return to the self-assured belief that the Easter faith is a story born of grief and despair, that a resurrected life is only the wish of those who dread the dampness of the tomb, or that the living Savior is only a fantasy of those who have no guts to live life on their own.

Living Christ, open our ears of faith that we, like Mary, might hear our names called. Even though the self-righteous saw her as unworthy, you, Forgiving One, gave her the privilege of knowing that you were victorious over the grave. Mary's life is the miracle of all those who believe that you are the resurrection and the life. You breathe into us a new spirit of faith, hope, and love. Your love does not disappoint us. The grave is not our end. It is a transition to a resurrected life where pain, suffering, and dying are no more. Christ, our Savior, is risen today. Allelujah.   *Amen.*

Easter Evening (A, B, C)

ISAIAH 25:6–9
PSALM 114

I CORINTHIANS 5:6b–8
LUKE 24:13–49

Amazing God, you swallow up death forever through the resurrection of your child, Jesus Christ. The bright hopes of this day of victorious life are sustained as the shadows of evening begin to steal across the sky.

Be present at the many evening meals set upon the tables of diverse peoples around the world. May a feast of bread and well-aged wines bring to mind the breaking of the bread, the blessing and the sharing of it at a village called Emmaus. May our eyes be opened to recognize Jesus as an ever-present guest at tables where bread and wine are given in Christ's name. Help us to see the abiding presence of our paschal lamb, who poured out the divine life as a blessing for all. Enable us to be generous with the food we earn through daily labor. Guide us in our sharing so that sincerity and truth will be transparent in the festival of our Savior.

As the sun sets on this Easter evening, may a bright star appear in the heavens. May the symbol of the star remind us of the hope we have through the Holy One of Easter. Blessed Jesus, sustain in us the patience to wait for you in the moment of life when light appears. Spread over all the nations the light of peacemaking. May the bright candle of peace not be blown out by the wild winds of ethnic cleansing or the easy promises of self-intent. Open our hearts to the profound promise of peace which Easter evening brings. May the uplifted words of Jesus bless the world with peace, and may all God's children sleep unafraid. *Amen.*

Second Sunday of Easter

ACTS 2:14a, 22–32   I PETER 1:3–9
PSALM 16   JOHN 20:19–31

Our hearts are glad, O God, for in your presence there is fullness of joy. Your great mercy has given us a new birth into a living hope through the resurrection of Jesus Christ. You are ruler of all the world and yet also our personal God whose counsel is always available and whose instruction can ever be found.

And yet we lock the doors of our lives to keep other people from knowing us, to keep those we consider different from changing us, to keep you at a distance for fear of surrendering what we think is under our control. We suffer trials alone rather than admitting our vulnerability. We struggle with doubts we dare not confess. Free us, O God, from the prisons of our own making that separate us from you and from one another.

We are thankful for the goodly heritage that draws us back to you and fills us with hope. We have no good apart from you. When we choose other gods, we multiply our sorrows. We bless you, O God, grateful that you are ever available to us. By your power, we are being saved. By your love, we are lifted up to indescribable and glorious joy.

We have good news to share. Show us how to make it real in our lives and relevant for others. Help us listen to their stories, understand their situations, and care about them in the fullness of your love. Keep us from thinking or acting as if our views are the only truth. Rather, let our lives point others to their own experience of Jesus Christ and an abiding trust in you. We pray in Jesus' name.   *Amen.*

Third Sunday of Easter

ACTS 2:14a, 36–41

PSALM 116:1–4, 12–19

I PETER 1:17–23

LUKE 24:13–35

Gracious God, we thank you for the trust we have gained through our risen Savior. Our faith and hope are focused on you and not on futile ways which perish. Even though we suffer distress and anguish, the old fears do not prevail. Our souls are at rest because you, O God, have dealt with us not according to our sins but according to the bounty of your mercy.

Abide with us as we center ourselves on Peter's proclamation concerning Jesus of Nazareth. May the power of Jesus' person so shape our lives that the light of the divine presence can be seen.

Listen carefully, Holy God, to our supplications. We pray for many of your children who fear the snares of death each day. Vain politicians seek to take breakfast off a child's table while they grow fat on corporate contributions. Fearful children can't go out to play because bullets made in America whiz by their ears while cowardly citizens clutch their weapons to their breasts. Why, O God, do we go on day after day believing the inane demonic prattle of talk show hosts? Our children are dying emotionally, educationally, physically, and spiritually. We deny them a future, O God, because we disobey the truth of your love and suffer media fools gladly. By your power, Holy One, open our minds to the truth of the Easter gospel. Quicken us to its claim and move us up from this grave of fear to the light of a resurrection morning. With this faith, move us with determination to reclaim the responsibilities of a citizenship which will serve the hopes of our children, and inspire us to lift them up as our living Savior did. May our amen be your call to action, O Resurrected One. *Amen.*

Fourth Sunday of Easter

ACTS 2:42–47   I PETER 2:19–25
PSALM 23   JOHN 10:1–10

Shepherd of all, we listen to your voice. It speaks to us when we attend to the teachings of the apostles. It assures us in the midst of suffering. It touches us when we break bread together with glad and generous hearts. Your presence is a continuing comfort to us. You accompany us through our times of trial and despair. You welcome us to the safety of your fold.

We confess that we have rebelled at times against your reign among us. We reject the green pastures and still waters for haunts that seem more exciting. We turn away from your table, seeking a menu more to our liking. We resent some of the other sheep of your fold and prefer not to associate with them. We have gone astray, responding to the voice of strangers. Then, when we find ourselves in difficulty, we wonder why it is so hard to make contact with you.

Thank you, God, for recalling us to your temple, meeting us in our homes, and speaking to us through friends. Thank you for the wonders and signs all around that reveal your creative hand and fill us with awe. Thank you for Jesus, who came to earth so that we might have life and have it abundantly.

Grant us the courage to follow where Jesus leads. Keep us honest and just, freeing us from our bondage to sin. Save us from abusive relationships, whether as victim or perpetrator. May we become channels of healing for others, as we ourselves are being healed. May we carry the good will of your people into relations of faithfulness. Surely goodness and mercy will follow us through life, and we will dwell with you forever.   *Amen.*

Fifth Sunday of Easter

ACTS 7:55–60
PSALM 31:1–5, 15–16

I PETER 2:2–10
JOHN 14:1–14

A strong fortress are you, mighty God. Come near to us and deliver us from the whirlwind of escalating violence. We stand at the edge of graves each day because we have freely surrendered our faith in you, O God, to the powers of this present age. Forgive us, O children and youth, that we bury your future because we have lost the courage to believe the gospel. Each day some of you die because we believe the demonic gospel of the gun lobby rather than the resurrection truth of Jesus Christ. Forgive us, O God, when we so easily believe rulers who claim to lead us to higher ground but use language of gutter rats. They claim to be leaders, yet they hold up tools minted from wealth meant to keep us in bondage to the pharaohs of our time.

You come, O risen Christ, to liberate us from our easy surrender to the smooth talk of party conversation. Save us, holy truth, from those whose oracles seek to have us turn aside from the healing power of an Easter faith. Equip us to stand firm in the way, the truth, and the life of Jesus Christ. Standing on the promises of the Risen One helps us to do the work which gives hope and life. We ask in your name, precious Savior, for the strength of will to overcome our willingness to seek our own interest and not the good of others. Let not our hearts be troubled by fears generated by messengers dealing in death. Let us believe in God and in our risen Savior. We come to you, Living One. In your name is our life, our hope, and our peace. Move us, Saving One, to be instruments of life, hope, and peace. *Amen.*

Sixth Sunday of Easter

ACTS 17:22–31
PSALM 66:8–20

I PETER 3:13–22
JOHN 14:15–21

Loving God, in whom we live and move and have our being, we bless you for keeping us among the living. We praise you for times of testing and moments of challenge. Through many trials, you have brought us out to a spacious place.

We confess that at times we have been more religious than faithful. We have kept up appearances of devotion while neglecting our prayers and faltering in our service. We fear what complete commitment might demand of us, so we try to be half-Christians. We limit our perceptions of who you are, mighty God, shaping you in our minds as One who fits our desires and needs. In our ignorance, we discount your judgment and fail your test. We repent of our selective responses to your love and our limited attention to the crying and desperate needs faced by so many of our sisters and brothers. Forgive us, we pray, and grant us a good conscience as we bow in honest humility before you.

Thank you for overlooking the many times when our human ignorance is so obvious. Thank you for accepting our prayers when they were little more than selfish cries or childish attempts at bargaining with you. We bring to you offerings of thankfulness. We seek to fulfill the vows we have made, those our mouths promised when we were in trouble. We bring you our love in response to your outpouring of care in the resurrection of Jesus and the gift of the Holy Spirit.

We bring to you our prayers for all to whom you are still unknown, for all who build barriers that divide instead of recognizing our common origin and destiny in you. We commit ourselves to testifying to the world of the hope that is in us. Keep us gentle and reverent in our defense of the gospel.   *Amen.*

Ascension of Jesus (A, B, C) (or Seventh Sunday of Easter)

ACTS 1:1–11

EPHESIANS 1:15–23

PSALM 47 OR PSALM 93

LUKE 24:44–53

Holy God, you continually call upon us to bless your name by being a blessing to others. You seek daily to open our minds to understand the truth of the scriptures. You constantly move us to repent of destructive ways of living. You stand by us moment by moment as we struggle to live in new life-giving ways. When we fall into old death-dealing patterns, you lift us up by your word of forgiveness. You rejoice with us as we find our way home to the joy of your promises.

Risen Savior, we thank you for your abiding presence in our lives and over the places where your people live. You ascended to the presence of our Creator so that you can continually guide us in the life-equipping power of the good news. Enrich our faith, Christ Jesus. May our believing be expressed in loving and just deeds which benefit all the peoples of creation.

Move us, ever-present Savior, to remember in our prayers all those who suffer unjustly the pains and the burdens of human conflicts. Open the eyes of our hearts that we can see their distress and be moved to participate in actions which can relieve their discomfort. Direct us, O God, to demonstrate through our giving the immeasurable greatness of your power through the good works of those who believe. Inspire us to greater capacities for service that the disordered lives of many of your people may be robed and girded with strength.

Gracious God, rule in our hearts and establish your purpose there. Then may an orderly compassion take hold of our minds that your saving ways may grasp and shape our daily living.

Let the people of faith say   *Amen.*

Seventh Sunday of Easter
Alternate

ACTS 1:6–14

I PETER 4:12–14, 5:6–11

PSALM 68:1–10, 32–35

JOHN 17:1–11

Awesome God, who gives strength and power to your people, we lift up songs of praise to honor you. Let the righteous be joyful. Let us exalt before you and be jubilant. You have gone before us through the wilderness. You have accompanied us through the storms of life. Your blessings have rained down upon us until we are engulfed in your love.

Yet your reign is not realized among us. We are impatient for conditions around us to change. We look for the transformation or destruction of the wicked. We want relief from the difficulties we face. We seek protection from evil and suffering. We expect you to act to save us. O God, when we listen to ourselves, we realize how selfish we are. We have not acted on the mandate we have received to witness to the ends of the earth. We have rebelled against the values Christ lived among us. We are not worthy of all your gifts to us. Turn us from the destructive paths we are following. Restore us to oneness with each other and with you, we pray.

We want to be open to your Holy Spirit. Grant us courage to accept our share of suffering for Christ's sake, for love compels us to offer acceptance and caring even to those who will reject it. Lift our anxiety so we may dare to reach out on behalf of sisters and brothers who are oppressed. Alert us to those places where our witness is needed, and grant us the humility to work with others in mutual regard and commitment. Guide us as we develop the self-discipline required to walk in the footsteps of Jesus. To Christ be the power forever and ever.   *Amen.*

Reflections

Pentecost and the
Season Following

Reflections

Day of Pentecost

ACTS 2:1–21 OR NUMBERS 11:24–30
PSALM 104:24–34, 35b

I CORINTHIANS 12:3b–13
JOHN 20:19–23 OR JOHN 7:37–39

Creating God, you send your Spirit to every spot in your universe to sustain your creative work. May your glory endure forever in the mystery of the molecule and the grandeur of the Milky Way. May your mercy thrive forever in the generosity of thoughtful children and in the great gifts of an abundant earth. Your universe, O God, sings songs of praise in the stars above and in the sounds of whales from the depths of the sea. May our meditations on the wonderful expression of your creative Spirit, divine Creator, be pleasing to you.

Open our minds, Redeeming One, to a fire of compassion which flames in our hearts. There in the deep reaches of the story of faith may we find the creative energy necessary to sustain the witness of the day of Pentecost. May the diverse languages we use to tell the story be as one in speaking the truth that Jesus Christ frees and unites. May the flame of the message of Jesus warm the cold hearts of those who have a hard time trusting anyone. May the light of the truth of our Savior open the eyes of those who surrender their lives to the danger of drugs. May the saving power of this Spirit heal each one of us of our predisposition to look out for ourselves first.

Let us rejoice in the presence of your Spirit, living God, for the variety of gifts you have given to humankind. Inspire us to use these many gifts for a manifestation of the Spirit for the common good. Quicken us to appropriate the use of our individual gifts for the restoration of a sense of a community of the Spirit.

Let the Spirit inspire our saying   *Amen.*

Trinity Sunday (First Sunday after Pentecost)

GENESIS 1:1–2:4a

PSALM 8

2 CORINTHIANS 13:11–13

MATTHEW 28:16–20

You alone, O God, have the capacity to create living beings on the face of the earth. Only you, O God, have the self-contained energy to explode, in an act of creative purpose, matter into a universe of light and shadow. By yourself, O God, have you sustained your creation from before time began until time shall be no more. Look and observe, people of God: from the depths of the sea to the expanse of the heavens, the Holy One speaks how our descendants were loved and disciplined and we are free.

Jesus, our Savior, you have authority in heaven and earth to guide us in the cleansing of nations through the water of baptism. Remind us, that our baptism is not our gift to give or withhold. It is you, O Spirit of Jesus, who call us in the washing of our baptism to take on the work of service. You give water to weary travelers for washing and healing. You present to us the wounds of the injured for cleansing and caring. You provide for us the destroyed homes of the homeless for repair and restoration. By the symbol of our baptism, Spirit of God, you have sealed us as a sign for an unclean world. You send us into the world to assist you in its cleansing. You wash it with pain, and it smells clean and refreshed. You teach us to keep your commandments and beatitudes, and the people find life ordered and blessed. You wash all people with love, and your baptized world gives itself for others through works of love.

Come, O God, Creator, Savior, and Holy Spirit. Wash the world with the waters of love and justice. Let the baptized of God say *Amen.*

Proper 4

Sunday between May 29 and June 4 (if after Trinity Sunday)

GENESIS 6:9–22; 7:24; 8:14–19   ROMANS 1:16–17; 3:22b–28, (29–31)

PSALM 46   MATTHEW 7:21–29

OR DEUTERONOMY 11:18–21, 26–28 OR PSALM 31:1–5, 19–24

O God, our refuge and strength, a very present help in trouble, we would be still before you, meditating on all your works. You have established your covenant with the people you have created. You have set us in families and communities for mutual support and encouragement so that all may come to know their own worth as your children. You offer salvation to all who turn to you in faith, trusting your mercy and seeking to live according to your will.

We have not always listened for that will nor sought to follow when we discern what you expect of us. We fill the earth with violence, whether by our overt acts against others, our wasteful misuse of resources, or our lack of compassion for those who need our care. When you judge us corrupt, we protest our innocence rather than examining our actions and motives. We have sinned against you and fall short of your glory. No amount of good we can do can take away our guilt or repay the debts we owe. Only you can restore us to a right relationship with you, Creator, and with all creation. Help us now, we pray.

Let your Word hold authority for us today, empowering us to live by faith. Reconcile us to one another, wiping out the weapons we use against our neighbors and leading us in new ways of mutual understanding. Reveal to us the gospel of your grace so that we may receive it with renewed commitment. We seek to build our lives and our communities on the firm foundation of your love, not on the quicksand of prejudice and self-interest. May your name be exalted among us.   *Amen.*

Proper 5

Sunday between June 5 and June 11

GENESIS 12:1–9   ROMANS 4:13–25
PSALM 33:1–12   MATTHEW 9:9–13, 18–26
OR HOSEA 5:15–6:6 OR PSALM 50:7–15

Righteous and just God, we gather in awe before you, celebrating your steadfast love and faithfulness. Your Word created the vast universe of time and space. The world and all that is in it belong to you. By your righteous intent, we have received the gift of life. O God, we glorify you and invoke your name.

Yet we forget to seek your face as each new day begins. We neglect the altars our ancestors built to honor you. Our love disappears like the morning dew. We become separated from you. This is the essence of sin we are reluctant to face. We cannot hear you because we are not expecting your Word or listening for it. We are more ready to kill your prophets than to heed their warnings. In our anxiety and distress, we need the Great Physician.

We reach out to touch the garment of salvation and are amazed that you look on us with favor. We would pay our vows to you in joyous gratitude. May the sacrifice of our thanksgiving become a mighty chorus, Gracious God, transforming our families, our church, our world. May we grow in faith as we accept your promises and receive your mercy. When we trust in you, we return to wholeness. Life emerges from death. Sorrow is overcome in the joy of your appearing.

Receive our prayers for those who have not heard of your grace, for all who waver in their commitments, for every person and group weighed down by troubles, for those whose wealth separates them from you, for all whose poverty leads to hopelessness and death. Equip us, as Christ's disciples and apostles, to listen, to follow, and to serve in ways that proclaim your faithfulness. May our lives reflect your love, and our lips pour forth praise from the depths of our being.   *Amen.*

Proper 6

Sunday between June 12 and June 18 (if after Trinity Sunday)

GENESIS 18:1–15, (21:1–7)   ROMANS 5:1–8

PSALM 116:1–2, 12–19   MATTHEW 9:35; 10:8, (9–23)

OR EXODUS 19:2–8a OR PSALM 100

Appear to us in these moments of prayer, amazing God, for we seek to find favor with you. Through our days, you have watched over us while we were unaware of your presence. You have inclined an ear to us even when we have silently ignored you. Your beauty has richly blessed us, far beyond any deserving. Hear us now as we seek to be conscious of who you are, so far exceeding our imagination.

O God, you know us better than we know ourselves. You understand our weakness. You are with us in times of sickness and distress. When we are harassed and helpless, you invite us to confide in you and depend on you. In our disappointment and times of grief, there is no greater comfort than your sustaining love. Your compassion for us we have observed in Jesus of Nazareth, whose life is our model, and whose death provides for our salvation.

We admit that we do not understand all this. Your grace is beyond our comprehension. Your promises stretch our belief. Your challenges call forth from us more than we knew was in us. You have summoned us as healers, as proclaimers of good news. You send us out to reap a plentiful harvest for Christ and the church.

We will call on you, O God, as long as we live. We will offer to you our thanksgiving sacrifices and pay our vows to you in the presence of a gathered congregation. Empower us with compassion for all who suffer that we may help them endure. Shape our character in ways that produce hope. We commit ourselves to living together in love, open to the Holy Spirit. *Amen.*

Proper 7

Sunday between June 19 and June 25 (if after Trinity Sunday)

GENESIS 21:8–21

PSALM 86:1–10, 16–17

ROMANS 6:1b–11

MATTHEW 10:24–39

OR JEREMIAH 20:7–13 OR PSALM 69:7–10, (11–15), 16–18

You are our God. Be gracious to us. Many of us are thrown out of our families because our parents are fussing over privilege. Like Hagar's son, we wander in the wilderness of desertion without a home. Our fathers are gone. O God, be a parent to us. Shelter us from pangs of poverty and the insecurity of an uncertain future. Preserve our lives, O God, for to you we cry all day long.

Give a hearing, precious Savior, in our day of trouble. We need you every hour to assure us that we will not be abandoned to the night. Teach us your way, O God, that we may walk in your truth. Give each one of us an undivided heart, so that we can honor your name. Receive our acts of devotion as feeble but honest efforts to revere the One who honors our efforts to persevere.

Deliver us, O God, from the war zone of domestic battles. We have struggled with our fathers and battled with our mothers. Our enemies feel like members of our household. Each day is a struggle with an accusing other. Aid us, dear God, to find a way out of the turmoil. Grant each one of us the capacity to surrender our self-righteousness on the altar of your purpose for us. Save us from the mean spirit of self-pity. Enliven us to a living hope of those who find their lives by losing them in your service. We turn to you, O Gracious One. Give strength to your servants, and save the lives of your parentless children. Show them a sign of your comfort and favor. Incline your ear toward them, O God, and answer them for the sake of the child of God who had no place to rest. *Amen.*

Proper 8

Sunday between June 26 and July 2

GENESIS 22:1–14

PSALM 13

ROMANS 6:12–23

MATTHEW 10:40–42

OR JEREMIAH 28:5–9 OR PSALM 89:1–4, 15–18

God of Easter mornings and the mysteries of life, you come as an angel. You are present in the thicket of life. When the hope of our life appears to be surrendered to the power of death, you arrive with a staying hand. As significant relationships test our sense of faithfulness, you hold us at the altar of promise. Here at the focus of worship and sacrifice, you call us to claim your promise, to sustain our hope, and to secure the future. Like Abraham and Isaac, we wonder if you know what you're doing on our terrible days. We anticipate the worst, yet in the moment of disaster you open a way for us to receive what you provide. Our hearts rejoice in your salvation, faithful God.

Open our hearts, Holy Spirit, that we may receive the One who is sent to sustain us on our journey of faith. Occasions to fall off the path of faithfulness come often. O God, strengthen us so that we do not yield ourselves to instruments of wickedness. Support us in our efforts to bear pain in our souls and sorrow in our hearts when the way is not clear and the outcome is clouded by our own anxiety. Help us to hold fast to a vision of your faithfulness, O God of promise. Direct us by the Light of the World, Jesus Christ. *Amen.*

Proper 8

Sunday between June 26 and July 2

GENESIS 22:1–14   ROMANS 6:12–23

PSALM 13   MATTHEW 10:40–42

OR JEREMIAH 28:5–9 OR PSALM 89:1–4, 15–18

How long will you hide from us, God of our ancestors? We look everywhere and cannot see you. We fly into space and you are not there, but a voice within tells us to listen and observe more closely, and gradually it dawns on us that you are everywhere. All life reveals your creative energy. You have dealt bountifully with us. Your steadfast love eases the pain in our souls and the sorrow in our hearts.

Forgive us when we misunderstand your expectations of us and act in ways that are harmful to others. Keep us from succumbing to the world's agenda and embracing lesser gods that beckon to us so temptingly. Save us from sin lest it exercise dominion over us. Let us not become instruments of wickedness. We have heard and believe that the wages of sin are death, but your free gift, through Jesus Christ, is eternal life.

May our lives ever flow with thanksgiving that matches your generous provision for our needs. We are grateful for the light you send and the assurance you give. We want to be obedient to all that Jesus is teaching us. As we enjoy the gift of freedom in Christ, we rededicate ourselves to the joyous task of welcoming others in Jesus' name. Open our eyes to see the needs around us and hear the cries of those who thirst for greater meaning in life than they have known. We want to offer cups of cold water where refreshment is needed and a warm embrace when loneliness prevails. We believe you will provide the resources we need to help our sisters and brothers along life's way. Thanks be to you, O God.

Amen.

Proper 9

Sunday between July 3 and July 9

GENESIS 24:34–38, 42–49, 58–67   ROMANS 7:15–25a
ZECHARIAH 9:9–12   MATTHEW 11:16–19; 25–30
OR PSALM 45:10–17 OR SONG OF SOLOMON 2:8–13 OR PSALM 145:8–14

We thank you, God, our mother and father, that you reveal yourself to children. We are grateful that your grandeur does not prevent you from entering the world of a child. In the playful rhymes of children, the revealing truth of our relationships is spoken in the light of day.

At high noon, O God, in the bright light, where there are no shadows to hide, we are portrayed as hypocrites. Children delightfully sing the truth of the pretentious privileges we claim for ourselves. In their subtle plays on words, we face the naked truth that many times we are not as we pretend to be. Create in us clean hearts, O God, and renew a wholesome spirit within us.

Grant unto us, O God, an obedient mind and a willing heart. May the hospitality of Rebekah be a witness to the transparent truth of gracious living. Help us to delight in the privilege of showing hospitality to your children. In moments of playful sharing, help us to experience the freedom of a joyous life lived in gratitude. Many acts of hospitality spring forth from a fountain of love. Let a spring of generosity flow in food for the hungry, justice for the oppressed, clothes for the naked, support for the weary, housing for the homeless, and education for the uninformed. Then may we experience the power of your hospitality toward us in the gift of Jesus Christ, your servant and our Savior.

Amen.

Proper 10

Sunday between July 10 and July 16

GENESIS 25:19–34   ROMANS 8:1–11

PSALM 119:105–112   MATTHEW 13:1–9, 18–23

OR ISAIAH 55:10–13 OR PSALM 65:(1–8), 9–13

In times of affliction and confusion, we come to you, O God. Life on this earth is not easy for your children. Often we feel internal conflict as we struggle between our desires and the highest values we know. Our flesh goes to war with our spirits, and the life of faith wrestles with the forces of death.

What is happening within us also seems to be occurring all around us. Nations are at war with one another. Factions within our country battle each other. There is division even within the church where we are called to realize our unity in Christ. Our homes become places of competition, distortion, and pain instead of havens where cooperation, honesty, and healing love abound.

We want all this to change, righteous God. We long for a life free from being constantly on guard lest someone take advantage of us. We desire a deeper understanding of your law and a fuller measure of your love penetrating all our days. We would walk, not according to the flesh, but by your Spirit, performing your statutes, and holding fast to your precepts. In union with the risen Christ, there is joy and peace. This is how we want to live.

O God, you have sowed seeds of love on this earth. Help us to be good soil in which all that you have planted can grow. May our lives be deeply rooted in your Word so we may endure times of trouble or persecution. Weed out the thorns of wealth and worldly care that threaten to choke the life out of us. We want to bear fruit for the expansion of your realm and the realization of your reign. *Amen.*

Proper 11

Sunday between July 17 and July 23

GENESIS 28:10–19a

PSALM 139:1–12, 23–24

ROMANS 8:12–25

MATTHEW 13:24–30, 36–43

OR WISDOM OF SOLOMON 12:13, 16–19 OR ISAIAH 44:6–8 OR PSALM 86:11–17

Lively God, you are the ongoing, meddling presence in our mundane lives. We stumble through much of our day not knowing whose world we're living in. At night we fall into bed with a sigh of relief. Thank God another day is over! We slumber into oblivion with our hand holding a hard-packed pillow. Thank you, faithful God, for a secure place to lay down our heads.

In the silence of the night, you come, O God, to bring our attention to a hope we do not see in the light of day. You enliven our sleep with the hopeful experience that surely God was in our day and we did not know it. We awake in awe and in confusion, surprised that our mundane day and the relief of sleep are the times when you bless us with your presence.

We are grateful, gracious God, for the sense of your abiding presence which assures us that we are your children. With childlike anticipation we look forward to the moments in life when our hopes are not disappointed. Continue to encourage us, Spirit of God, by the affirmation that, as children of our creator, we are heirs to a lively hope through Christ's resurrection.

Sustain, Compassionate One, all those who suffer the slings and arrows of life's outrageous fortunes. Uphold them in their hope that the sufferings of this time are not worth comparing to your love, which empowers us. Lay your holy hands upon those who suffer. Quicken them to sense the touch of your compassion. In the shadows of the evening, uplift them with the precious thought: When we awake, we are still with you. *Amen.*

Proper 12

Sunday between July 24 and July 30

GENESIS 29:15–28

PSALM 105:1–11, 45b OR PSALM 128

ROMANS 8:26–39

MATTHEW 13:31–33, 44–52

OR I KINGS 3:5–12 OR PSALM 119:129–136

We come to this time of prayer, O God of the ages, as on a venture of discovery. We are drawn by your holiness. We are attracted by love that will not let us go. We long for a relationship in which we not only receive but also become responsible partners. You have offered us a covenant, a relationship we can trust. We want to be trustworthy partners.

We bring to you our weaknesses, our impatience, our tendency to be distracted by many things. The mustard seed of faith has not found fertile soil within us. The yeast of your realm has missed among us the warm environment needed for expansive growth. We have not wanted your reign among us enough to center our lives on its pursuit. We are busy with so many things. So much is demanded of us as we try to make a living that we forget to live. We fail to approach everyday decisions and long-term planning from the viewpoint of our relationship with you.

Come, Holy Spirit, to awaken our awareness. Nothing can separate us from the love of God in Jesus Christ, our Savior. You are always present. Your guidance is always available. No human deceits have lasting power. No human failure is unredeemable. We give thanks to you, O God, and sing praises to you. Our hearts rejoice in your presence and celebrate your wonderful works.

All we receive is meant to be shared. We know that, God. Your reign is realized only in community. Help us to be catalysts of love in your realm, welcoming others into covenant relationship with you. Teach us in this hour what you would have us do. *Amen.*

Proper 13

Sunday between July 31 and August 6

GENESIS 32:22–31   ROMANS 9:1–5

PSALM 17:1–7, 15   MATTHEW 14:13–21

OR ISAIAH 55:1–5 OR PSALM 145:8–9, 14–21

O God of our parents in faith, you visit us in the night when the hustle of the day quiets down. We call to you, for you will hear and respond to us. Hear the great sorrow and unceasing anguish in our hearts, Faithful One. We are troubled by the divisions in our own household of faith. We belong to the same family, and yet we are constantly picking at the places where we're hurting. We wrestle not with angels, O God, for we are preoccupied with our own righteousness. We observe the limping in the lives of others and fail to see the wreck we make of our own lives. Let our eyes see the right that you see, Holy One. Then call to mind how we have slipped from your path. Direct our eyes and minds to the wonders of your steadfast love for each one of us in the household. In the experience of your love, awaken us to your blessing of a relationship of promise.

Draw us together, generous God, in the deed of spreading a tablecloth where all can be included and fed. May the reality of the thoughtfulness of Christ inspire in us the spirit of sharing. Enable us to open our hands in the gift of giving. Open our minds to the truth that in giving we receive, in forgiving we find release, and in breaking the bread and passing the cup our sense of separateness is swallowed up in the fullness of Christ's life. For in our Savior's face we see God, and our lives are preserved. Let the people of faith awake and be satisfied with beholding the face of God in the glory of Jesus Christ. *Amen.*

Proper 14

Sunday between August 7 and August 13

GENESIS 37:1–4, 12–28   ROMANS 10:5–15
PSALM 105:1–6, 16–22, 45b   MATTHEW 14:22–33
OR I KINGS 19:9–18 OR PSALM 85:8–13

God of all nations and all people, we have heard your summons to us. Through stormy days, we hear your call. When the fragile boat of life sails the restless seas, your voice reaches us amid crashing waves as a whisper within our souls. We catch glimpses of your presence in the midst of our panic, and we cry out: Save us, O God.

We confess that we become so focused on our own plight that we find it difficult to identify with the experience of sisters and brothers whose situations are more desperate than our own. Indeed, it becomes easier to view them as enemies than as next of kin. When we see them as threats, it is hard to welcome them in love. They become expendable commodities rather than embraceable comrades. There are many ways of selling others into second-class citizenship. We are guilty of letting this happen.

Once more, we ask forgiveness of you, forgiving God. In the name of Jesus Christ, save us and help us to believe. You are generous to all who call on you. Hear us now. Even as we ask you to hear us, our ears are opened to good news of salvation.

We give thanks to you, O God, and tell of your wonderful works. We will make your ways known among the people we meet. We will tell of your wisdom and freeing Spirit. O God, we are ready to go where you send us. We are ready to tell the world of your love for all, in Jesus Christ our Savior. We commit ourselves anew to the practical hard work of changes that will bring all your children to first-class participation in your realm.   *Amen.*

Proper 15

Sunday between August 14 and August 20

GENESIS 45:1–15   ROMANS 11:1–2a, 29–32
PSALM 133   MATTHEW 15:(10–20), 21–28

OR ISAIAH 56:1, 6–8 OR PSALM 67

Merciful One, through the mysteries of history you craft our shameful
deeds and dirty tricks into mirrors of self-encounter and self-discovery. Our own
sins find us out and throw up in our faces the shadow side of our selves. Our
own disobedience to your love has delivered us to a day of disasters. Yet in this
time of painful discovery, Unsearchable One, you call forth the graciousness of
the ones whom we sought to destroy.

Help us, O God, not to run away from the time of painful self-disclosure.
Enable us to stand in the moment when those we have injured will say: "I am
your brother, your sister, your child. Do not be distressed or angry with
yourselves. God sent me before you to preserve for you a time to be alive."
Merciful God, equip us with a courage that can not only claim the truth found
in self-discovery but can also embrace those who show us mercy.

Deliver us all, O God, from a time of mean-spirited living. The spirit of
this age has gripped us. It always asks: "Where is mine?" It continually boasts:
"It is mine." We hang on to our stuff without mercy. We claim more than we
need because we want abundance. Joseph's brothers wanted more, and they
reaped a famine of hope and a whirlwind of fear. Move us back, faithful God,
from the brink of disaster to the bounty of your sustaining grace. Aid us in our
acceptance of the amazing generosity of persons who give out of gratitude. In
our astonishment, of their mercy, move us to accept your expectation of us. Let
us hear your expectation: I provided for you in the day of famine, for you and all
your household. Therefore, share that no more poverty shall be in the land. May
a generous people say   *Amen.*

Proper 16

Sunday between August 21 and August 27

EXODUS 1:8–2:10   ROMANS 12:1–8
PSALM 124   MATTHEW 16:13–20

OR ISAIAH 51:1–6 OR PSALM 138

You are ever at our side, gracious God. We pause to recognize that we are in your presence. In all times and places, you are our help and our deliverer. When we conform too much to this world, you show us that there is more to life than pursuit of our own gain. When we seek to shore up our self-esteem with inflated views of our own importance, you redirect us to excellence, not superiority over others.

Today we bring to you our concern for people who live in oppressive and threatening situations: for children existing on the streets of our cities, for families huddled in fear where bullets fly, for youth caught in a culture of drugs and promiscuity, for workers exploited in dangerous occupations, for all who find themselves in bondage like the Hebrews in Egypt. We pray for them as a first step toward addressing their plight in other ways.

May our church become, ever more effectively, a center for healing and transformation. Renew our minds so we may think clearly about issues, situations, and persons, seeking to discern your will. As your purposes become clearer to us, help us to act wisely for the good of all. Unite us as members of one body in which each part is important. May each of us use our individual gifts for the common benefit and in outreach to a needy world. Let us not fear to be living sacrifices, devoting ourselves to the causes you place before us.

Draw us ever closer to you in faith and trust. Guide our proclamation of Jesus as Messiah and Savior. May we grow in discipleship, that our church might be a center of faith and faithfulness for many.   *Amen.*

Proper 17

Sunday between August 28 and September 3

EXODUS 3:1–15   ROMANS 12:9–21

PSALM 105:1–6, 23–26, 45c   MATTHEW 16:21–28

OR JEREMIAH 15:15–21 OR PSALM 26:1–8

Visiting God, through our hearing of the cries of persons in distress you visit us. You come to us in the cries of terror from children and women who are enslaved in households of brutality. You call out from the flames of battlefields where human life cries out in its last breath. You come visiting us, O God, where persecution, oppression, and cursing are the currency of the day. Ever-present God, help us to hear the cries, but also aid us to hear your voice as it says: "Come here. See and follow my command."

Expecting God, we honestly admit that we're like Moses. We have a need for an amazing sign that you are really making a claim on us. Cries far away as well as those close by make us uneasy. Every cry is a call for a costly rescue. Every scream in the night is an invitation to trouble. God, give us a name that the cries of the world will recognize. Give us a powerful sign that the powers of this world will see and surrender to. Forgive us, Strong Deliverer, for our easy acknowledgment of ineptitude for the call and our inability to face the fires of our time. Taking up the cross of justice has within it an uncertain future. How, O God, will the powers of injustice listen to an inarticulate few? The Holy One says this to us: "Those of you who would save your lives will lose them, and those who lose their lives for my sake will find them. For what advantage will it be to gain the whole world and forfeit one's life?"

Liberating God, strengthen us to call on your name. Empower us to make known your purpose among nations. Help us to sing out the song of justice, and enable us to carry its cross with joy. Remembering the wonderful works that God is doing, let the people say   *Amen.*

Proper 18

Sunday between September 4 and September 10

EXODUS 12:1–14   ROMANS 13:8–14

PSALM 149   MATTHEW 18:15–20

OR EZEKIEL 33:7–11 OR PSALM 119:33–40

We gather every Sunday in a festival of remembrance and celebration. Week after week, our meeting is much the same, yet each occasion is unique. Every experience of worship offers us the opportunity for new beginnings. So we come to you today, Loving God, in eager anticipation of a season of renewal and growth. In the name of Jesus Christ, we lift our prayers.

We praise you, O God, for times of deliverance. You have granted us moments of victory in the midst of losses. We have known times of triumph when all appeared lost. You seem to take pleasure in us, even when we are down on ourselves. We praise you with words and songs, with dance and drama, and with lives open to your judgment and correction.

Your law calls for our answering love. We admit that we are often far from loving in our words and deeds. We bend your commandments to suit our whims. Forgive, we pray, those who admit their unfaithfulness. Forgive us for claiming as our due more than our share of the world's resources. No matter how much we have, we seem inclined to covet even more rather than share what we have. Help us to grow in both understanding and practice of what it means to love our neighbors as ourselves. Lead us to live honorably as disciples of Jesus Christ.

Bless, we pray, the ministry and mission of this congregation. Grant that we may live and work together in harmony, not out of sameness, but through listening and with a growing understanding of differences. Whenever two or three of us get together, let us sense your presence and pause to thank you. In Jesus' name. *Amen.*

Proper 19

Sunday between September 11 and September 17

EXODUS 14:19–31　　　　　　　　　　　　　ROMANS 14:1–12
PSALM 114 OR EXODUS 15:1b–11, 20–21　　　MATTHEW 18:21–35
OR GENESIS 50:15–21 OR PSALM 103:(17), 8–13

God of our weary years, God of our silent tears, lead us through the deep waters of life. Every evening we see and hear an ever-increasing wail of destruction waiting to drown our way of life. Streets are dangerous. Homes are ripped by violence. Schools are unsafe places. Legislative halls are cesspools of self-interest. The waters are getting higher, our feet are weary of walking, and our voices are drowned out in the parade of perpetual chatter. We don't know who to listen to because every voice is selling us a bill of goods.

Truth-telling God, come with your light to clear our muddled minds of the deceptive claims of contemporary political hucksters. Stretch out your hands and draw us into the sea of your truth. Open our eyes to see and our ears to hear that words of ridicule and deceit are waves of destruction.

Send us, freeing God, the clarity of your presence each day so that we can claim that none of us lives to ourselves, and none of us dies to ourselves. Sustain us in the affirmation that we travel on your path with our sisters and brothers. Guide us when the uncertain moments of history are causing us to hesitate. Grant us courage to stand on the rock of your promised presence. Move us to seek your purpose in the sanctuary of truthfulness. Stay our hearts from the subtle seduction of deceptive promising. Encourage us to join hands with those who, in faith, walk in the deep waters of life. May our wading in the waters wash our minds and hearts clear for faithful service. Let all who believe shout

Amen.

Proper 20

Sunday between September 18 and September 24

EXODUS 16:2–15   PHILIPPIANS 1:21–30

PSALM 105:1–6, 37–45   MATTHEW 20:1–16

OR JONAH 3:10–4:11 OR PSALM 145:1–8

In these quiet moments, away from our busy routines, we seek your presence, glorious God. Our hearts rejoice as we feel touched by your love and care. Our ancestors in the faith have testified to your wonderful works. You led them out of slavery, rained bread from heaven to feed them when they were hungry, and guided them by cloud and fire through the desert. You gave them laws to guide them and kept your promises to them so that they sang for joy.

Yet they were not content with their lot. They complained when life was difficult, forgetting all the ways you had helped them. They became envious of one another when it seemed that some were favored more than others. There are times when we, too, wonder why good people suffer and evil seems to triumph. We are not eager to share the good you provide with people who seem not to have worked as hard as we have. Why should undeserving people receive as much of your love as we do? Forgive our greed and jealousy, lest they consume us, O God.

Help us to live in a manner worthy of the gospel of Christ. Unite us so that we may serve side-by-side with common devotion to the One Spirit. Grant us courage, not only to serve but to suffer, if need be, that your will may be accomplished among us. May we offer hospitality to strangers and a genuine welcome to all your children, not because they are like us, but because they are loved by you and kin to us through Christ.   *Amen.*

Proper 21

Sunday between September 25 and October 1

EXODUS 17:1–7   PHILIPPIANS 2:1–13
PSALM 78:1–4, 12–16   MATTHEW 21:23–32
OR EZEKIEL 18:1–4, 25–32 OR PSALM 25:1–9

You are among us, liberating God, whether we know it or not. When life
is a happy breeze, we bathe ourselves in its bounty. If hard times arrive because
we sold out to the joys of living, then we come moaning to you. We forget
what you have done, O God. Your miracle of life itself is forgotten. We pray for
an easy rescue from our self-made mess. "O God, save us painlessly," we pray.
In the wilderness of the desert, amazing God, you wash away our bitterness and
our forgetfulness. You give us water to quench our thirst. You summon us to
hold fast to the living water of your promise.

Deliver us, O God, from our ready compulsion to repeat the same old cycle
of forgetfulness when life abundantly blesses us. Forgive us when we neglect our
covenant with you. Awaken in us the capacity to recall how we test you in our
hearts. Renew in us the remembrance of your compassionate heart when you
forgave our iniquity. With thanksgiving, we bring to mind your restraint of
your own anger.

Help us to cultivate the mind of Christ among us. Move us to encourage the
growth of a wholesome incentive of love. Center us in a thought of your work
within and among us. Melt away conceit and self-interest, and restore in us an
openness to regard others as co-workers in discovering our mutual worth in your
sight. Enable us to believe that the simple acceptance of our common humanity in
Christ grants us the gift of equality that even death cannot take away.

Gracious God, continue to lead us as we work out our salvation with fear
and trembling. Continue your work within us, and form us into the likeness of
human beings worthy of your love. In the name of the exalted Christ, we
pray.   *Amen.*

Proper 22

Sunday between October 2 and October 8

EXODUS 20:1–4, 7–9, 12–20   PHILIPPIANS 3:4b–14
PSALM 19   MATTHEW 21:33–46

OR ISAIAH 5:1–7 OR PSALM 80:7–15

The heavens are telling your glory, mighty God, and the firmament proclaims your handiwork. Day-to-day pours forth speech, and night-to-night declares knowledge. All creation speaks to us without words and moves us without sound. We feel the warmth of the sun and are reminded of your care.

From generations past, we have received your law. You call us away from idols that distract us. You remind us that you are to be worshiped, not exploited for our selfish purposes. You direct us to observe sabbath times for refreshment and renewal. We confess that we have not loved you with all our hearts, souls, strength, and mind.

You lead us away from anger and exploitation in our relationships with other people. We know that murder, adultery, and robbery are grievous sins against ourselves as well as against those who are victims. Coveting and false witness destroy our integrity. Yet, how easy it is to slip into sins that separate us from you and one another. How tempting it is to rebel against parents and against you. We tremble before your judgment and beg your forgiveness. Cleanse us of hidden faults.

We come to you today, reigning God, through faith in Jesus Christ. We are amazed at the faithfulness to your love that Jesus lived. We are awed by the power of the resurrection to transform lives, including our own. We want to know Christ in our daily lives. We press on toward the goal for the prize of the heavenly call of God in Christ Jesus. Do not let us deny or betray this One who amazes us and invites us to live in your realm, beginning here and now. Accept us, we pray.   *Amen.*

Proper 23

Sunday between October 9 and October 15

EXODUS 32:1–14   PHILIPPIANS 4:1–9
PSALM 106:1–6, 19–23   MATTHEW 22:1–14

OR ISAIAH 25:1–9 OR PSALM 23

In the searing light of bright fall days, O God, our patience grows thin, and our perspective on life gets hazy. We take off our gold to buy idols of comfort and ease. We rise up early to buy symbols of well-being, and at high noon we sit down to eat and drink. Always seeking the easy way out from life's discomforts, we dull our awareness of the struggle to live faithfully with you, Holy God.

Forgive us, O God, that we, like our ancestors in faith at Mt. Sinai, create images to worship which have no life-giving or life-sustaining energy within them. Aid our understanding that we might recover a vision of the Living One, Jesus Christ our Savior. Help us to find true companionship with those who labor side-by-side with us to strengthen our faith in the One who keeps promises and remembers us in the sanctuary.

We call to mind all our sisters and brothers who have anxiety about bread, work, and shelter. Receive our supplication on their behalf, and shape us and them into a community of common concern. With thanksgiving to you, Generous One, we ask you to guide our efforts to overcome the structures which lead to hunger, unemployment, and homelessness. Let our requests made known to you be our inspiration to work for a society mindful of your interest in the benefit of all. Move us to go to the streets and gather together all who may be found. Sustain in us your invitation to each one of us to receive one another as guests at your feast. As we delight in the experience of joy in your celebration, joyous God, may we receive the peace which passes all understanding. Keep our hearts and minds in Christ Jesus.   *Amen.*

Proper 24

Sunday between October 16 and October 22

EXODUS 33:12–23   I THESSALONIANS 1:1–10

PSALM 99   MATTHEW 22:15–22

OR ISAIAH 45:1–7 OR PSALM 96:1–9, (10–13)

God of grace and glory, how great and awesome is your name. Before you, we tremble in eagerness and fear. You are a living and true God beside whom our foolish idols pale with insignificance. You form light and create darkness. All honor, strength, majesty, and beauty are in your hands.

Show us your ways, O God, and remind us of what you expect of us. We have encountered you as a lover of justice. Forgive us for the times we have acted unjustly and the occasions we have failed to speak or act when doing so could have made a difference. Pardon our deceitful ways meant to entrap those we consider enemies. Link us instead in prayer and labors of love. We mean to render to you what is rightfully yours, and to regard our neighbors with impartiality. Help us, Holy God.

Thank you for answering us when we call on you. Sometimes we long for insights. At these times, the way we should go is quickly apparent. The message of the gospel comes to us through the written Word but also through the Holy Spirit. We are empowered and come to full conviction as we wait on you. You have chosen us as ambassadors of good news.

Strengthen us, we pray, in the use of all our varied gifts for the sake of sisters and brothers who resist Christ's way of love. Rescue us from hypocrisy. Help us to be advocates for justice and fairness before those who would deny these opportunities to some. Help us to model responsibility and equity within the church and out in the world. Reign among us that we may become instruments of your perfect will. *Amen.*

Proper 25

Sunday between October 23 and October 29

DEUTERONOMY 34:1–12   I THESSALONIANS 2:1–8

PSALM 90:1–6, 13–17   MATTHEW 22:34–46

OR LEVITICUS 19:1–2, 15–18 OR PSALM 1

You wander with us, O God, through many years of searching and frequent nights of whys. By day, you provide a cloud of witnesses to guide. In the night, you give the fire of vision to inspire our willingness to press on to the place of promise. You stand by us when the self-satisfied keepers of tradition test and question our passion to move forward with the promise of the spirit. You visit us with your assuring presence, and we sense that our hope is not in vain. We find that the appeal of your future, O God, is more promising than the grand designs of scheming disciples of greed.

God of steadfast love and mercy, you have been our dwelling place in all generations. Before we were born, you watched over us. You have observed us struggling to reach a better place. We have come very far by faith, yet we worry that we will not make it to Jordan's side. Our years in life feel like they are numbered. They spin with toil and trouble, and years fly by, and our lives are soon gone. Holy God, will we only see the other side and, like Moses, not cross over? Stay with us, Author of Life, whether we simply see the vision or when we dance in the sanctuary of your presence. Teach us to appreciate the gift of our days, and may we get a heart of wisdom.

Living God, may our sense of life's limits hold for us no regrets. May the spirit of Moses and Paul and Zipporah and Phoebe sustain our appreciation of the journey of faithfulness. Deepen our sense of confidence in your promise that where you are, there we will be. Let a hopeful people say   *Amen.*

Proper 26

Sunday between October 30 and November 5

JOSHUA 3:7–17   I THESSALONIANS 2:9–13
PSALM 107:1–7, 33–37   MATTHEW 23:1–12
                    OR MICAH 3:5–12 OR PSALM 43

We draw near to hear you speaking to us, O God, through human speech
and in moments of quiet. You are always among us, whether we acknowledge
you or not. You are living and working in us, and in spite of us. You gather us
now from the east and the west, the north and the south to remember our
covenant with you.

Like our spiritual ancestors, we have wandered in the desert wastes, finding
no way to fulfilling encounters with you. We hunger and thirst for meaning,
and we chase many illusions in our search for satisfaction. All we find apart from
you is brackish waters and moldy bread. O God, we confess that our schemes do
not satisfy. Our lesser loyalties leave us empty. Our pretensions of faithfulness to
you are exposed as fraud. Turn us around. Unite heads, hearts, and wills in
honest devotion and service.

Teach us not only where to find truth, but let it also become a part of us.
May we live the faith in ways that do not so much call attention to us as point
beyond us to the Christ we seek to serve. Turn us away from the pursuit of
honors, privilege, or advantage. Keep us humble in our serving that our urging
and encouraging may show genuine care and our thankfulness attract others to
your love.

We pour out our thanks for your steadfast love that endures forever. We
have been delivered from distress and led along a straight way. You provide
springs of living water to refresh us. You bless us with abundance. You
empower us to witness effectively to a world that needs joyous good news and
practical help. When you send us, we will go.   *Amen.*

Proper 27

Sunday betweeen November 6 and November 12

JOSHUA 24:1–3a, 14–25   I THESSALONIANS 4:13–18

PSALM 78:1–7   MATTHEW 25:1–13

OR AMOS 5:18–24 OR PSALM 70

Holy God, you call us from beyond our secure locations to the security of your faithfulness. You encourage us to leave behind preferred religiosity to serve you in honesty and sincerity. You demand that we choose between the idols of purchased power and the holy God who sets the people free. Today you call: What's it going to be—indentured enslavement to petty powers or the only One with the power to wake the dead.

Deliver us, O God, from ongoing unpreparedness for your coming. When life suddenly gets tense, we foolishly want to borrow from others what we need to ready ourselves. We wait until the last stroke of midnight to engage ourselves for the coming of your Holy One. Why, dear God, do we always need a person such as Joshua to focus our attention that God is present and the moment to decide is now? Forgive our ignorant slumbering with the truth that you come to bless and comfort each day. Open our ears to the trumpet of God, which can awaken us to the reality that Jesus Christ is the promise of a risen life.

Give ear, O my people, says our God. Listen with your heart, not only your ears, to the speech of the Holy One. The Saving One delivered us from many dangers, renewed us from diverse moments of depression, and restored us to joyous times of embrace and celebration. Thank you, God, for staying true to your covenant with us. We praise you, Compassionate One, for forgiving our iniquity and delivering us from the fear of dying.

Direct our serving of your purpose through acts of compassion. With faithfulness to your promise, guide us in our faithfulness toward our neighbor. Let the faithful say   *Amen.*

Proper 28
Sunday between November 13 and November 19

JUDGES 4:1–17   I THESSALONIANS 5:1–11
PSALM 123   MATTHEW 25:14–30
OR ZEPHANIAH 1:7, 12–18 OR PSALM 90:1–8, (9–11), 12

We lift our eyes to the heavens, gracious God, seeking the mercy you so richly provide. When we are met in our daily efforts with scorn and contempt, you provide encouragement and acceptance. When there is only night around us, you come to us as light. When wrath and destruction descend on us, you provide a peace and security this world cannot give. Let us live with you in the community of faith, where we may learn to encourage and build up one another in love.

You have blessed us, O God, with many talents. Some we refuse to recognize. Some we hoard and hide. We are afraid to use these talents, lest our efforts be judged inferior. We hesitate to employ our talents with all their creative potential lest we call attention to ourselves. We look at others who seem to have been given so much more than we received, and we are envious. Why, O God, do you keep giving them more and more? Would you call us wicked and lazy just because we disguise our abilities rather than discharge our duties? Is that fair?

Who are we to judge you, God of light? Our laments say more about us than about you. Help us, O God, to equip ourselves with faith and love and the hope of salvation. Empower us to risk using to their fullest the gifts you entrust to us. Grant us the capacity to appreciate the efforts of others, to encourage them and build them up, to rejoice at their successes, and to share their disappointments.

Your day, O God, is at hand, and your judgments are just. Every day is precious in your sight. Teach us to count our days with appreciation for the opportunities they present. May we gain wisdom as we employ the gifts you have given.   *Amen.*

Proper 29 (Reign of Christ)

Sunday between November 20 and November 26

EZEKIEL 34:11–16, 20–24   EPHESIANS 1:15–23
PSALM 100   MATTHEW 25:31–46
OR EZEKIEL 34:11–16, 20–24 OR PSALM 95:1–7a

Mighty God, you called our Savior, Jesus Christ, out of the tomb. You raised Christ up as a symbol that your steadfast love endures forever. Our Redeemer's presence we celebrate in all generations through the breaking of bread and the sharing of the cup of blessing. To you we belong, O God. We are your people whom you have gathered from the scattered places of your world. You seek us out, Holy Shepherd, for the frenzy of our time fades our vision of your presence. You call us to serve you with gladness. We come into your presence with hymns of praise.

The joy of your presence, O precious Savior, calls to mind the needs of our sisters and brothers. Enrich their lives with the knowledge of your love. Empower their vision to see the manifestations of your presence in the daily routines of life. Enfold their loved ones with your embrace through the mystery of their own loving. Blessed Jesus, in the fullness of your ministry, the lives of many are filled to overflowing. May your generous blessing of our lives be the springboard to a generous giving of our lives in strengthening others. Grant to each of us a grateful heart which is always open to the need of another. May feeding the hungry, clothing the naked, visiting the oppressed, sheltering the homeless, and welcoming the unfamiliar be spontaneous acts of loving you, our neighbor, and ourselves. Infuse a spirit of generosity so deeply into our habits that we cannot remember any deed of kindness consciously given. May a generous people of God joyously say   *Amen.*

Reflections

Reflections

Special Days

Reflections

Presentation (A, B, C)

February 2

MALACHI 3:1–4

PSALM 84 OR PSALM 24:7–10

HEBREWS 2:14–18

LUKE 2:22–40

You, O Creator, have created a splendid dwelling place for all your creatures. Even the sparrows find your holy places ideal sites to build nests. O God of hosts, revive in us the joy of a swallow when it finds the beauty of your sacred space. Send your messenger to awaken us to the delight of your covenant promise. Come, appear with a cleansing fire and purify us of all that hinders an openness to receiving your welcome.

Blessed Jesus, move us to a childlike anticipation of your joy as we enter the sanctuary of blessing. May the knowledge of your parents' presentation of you to God move us to give ourselves anew to our divine parent. May the insight of Simeon into the mystery of your future as Messiah open our hearts to the meaning of your ministry for us. Help the church and each one of us to purify our mission in life at the altar of sacrificial giving. Sustain a spirit of presenting ourselves as instruments of service to a self-serving world. Open our minds and our souls to opportunity to grow in wisdom and in favor with you, welcoming God.

Give birth in us, embracing God, an attitude of genuine trust in your love for us so that we can continually be a people of hospitality in an unwelcoming world. May the stranger be received with joy in the sanctuary. Let all God's children rejoice in the dwelling place of God. May all those who find the day in this sacred place of presentation a blessing say   *Amen.*

Visitation (A, B, C)

May 31

I SAMUEL 2:1–10
PSALM 113

ROMANS 12:9–16b
LUKE 1:39–57

God of knowledge, you visit us in life's moments of anticipation and surprise. With Hannah and Mary, we are in awe of your visitation. Quicken our minds to receive your news with acceptance and with joy. May we rejoice in God our Savior with an expectation that history's haunting mystery will be illumined in the gift of Mary.

Child of God named Jesus, send your Spirit among us. Guard the journey of your faithful ones that your name might be praised from the sun's rising to its setting. Visit our time with your compassion that the meanness of spirit toward the poor and parentless might be judged in the court of the Merciful One.

Holy God, your glory is above the highest heaven. Yet you draw near to raise the poor from the dust. Lift the needy from the heap of ashes where pretentious politicians consign them. Help us be devoted to one another in a ministry of helpfulness. Move us to outdo one another in showing honor toward all who fall prey to the misfortunes of life. Strengthen us to gently call to account all those who exploit the generosity of others so that they can rest easy on life's journey.

Open our eyes to see in the needs of another the visitation of your call to mercy. Open our ears to hear in the cry of a hungry child your whisper: "Feed my lambs." Open our hearts to feel in the murmur of the dying your affirmation: "Creator, into your hands I commit my spirit."

Redeeming God, with your visitation, we rejoice in our hope. We are patient in tribulation and constant in prayer, and we practice hospitality. Take these gifts of affirmation and use them in your serving. Let a hopeful people say   *Amen.*

Holy Cross

September 14

NUMBERS 21:4b–9

PSALM 98:1–5 OR PSALM 78:1–2, 34–38

I CORINTHIANS 1:18–24

JOHN 3:13–17

Crucified Savior, you were lifted up on a tree to die a painful death, yet you conquered in your dying the foolish trash-talk of the wise and the silly conversations of the debaters of this world. The wisdom of your life, living Savior, is not that of the powerful noble-born. The source of your wisdom, Christ Jesus, is the One who gives life to all.

Help us sing a new song to the God of all wisdom. Dwell with us, Knowing One, as we marvel in the cross, in the old rugged cross. May we be inspired by the sense of victory. "It is finished." These words move us to experience with our Savior the mystery of the cross. Dear Jesus, we know God is the source of our life. Keep us close to the wisdom of the cross even when it is called foolishness by the rulers of the age.

High upon the cross, Holy Child of God, you saw all the nations of the world. You experienced their petty claims of sovereignty which lead to pain and suffering for many. You heard their prejudicial sense of superiority which leads to conflict and chaos. You witnessed their obsession with suspicion which causes some to die and others to be disgraced. Come, sovereign Savior, and show forth God's love for the world. God comes to redeem the world, not to condemn it. Let each one of us believe God's love and not perish. Receive the gift of God's eternal life. Let the people of God rejoice in the cross of Christ towering over the wrecks of time. Let the victorious people of God say *Amen.*

All Saints'

November 1 or the First Sunday in November

REVELATION 7:9–17   I JOHN 3:1–3
PSALM 34:1–10, 22   MATTHEW 5:1–12

Gather us with all your saints, O God, that we may join in the chorus of praise: "Salvation belongs to our God who is seated on the throne, and to the Lamb. Blessing and glory and wisdom and thanksgiving and honor and power and might be to our God forever and ever. Amen." We worship you with all we have and all we are, for you provide springs of the water of life to quench our thirst. You wipe the tears from our eyes. When we are hungry, you satisfy us with good things and deliver us from our fears. O taste and see that God is good. Look to our Creator and be radiant. All who take refuge in God will find their lives redeemed by love.

Thank you, God, for accepting us as your children and encouraging our growth. Purify us day by day to become more and more like Christ. Show us what it means to be pure in spirit, participating here and now in your realm. Comfort us in the midst of our mourning. Fill us with the righteousness for which we hunger and thirst. Grant us boldness to be merciful to others as you have been merciful to us. Bestow such purity of heart that we may see you, God. We would be peacemakers, even when we are unjustly persecuted. Keep us from returning evil for evil or responding defensively before false witness. We are glad and rejoice that we can be representatives of the risen Christ.

What we seek for ourselves, we would also offer to the world through all we meet. Knit us together in faithfulness so that generations to come may set their hopes on you, keep your commandments, and remember your works. *Amen.*

Thanksgiving Day

Fourth Thursday in November (U.S.) or Second Monday in October (Canada)

DEUTERONOMY 8:7–18   2 CORINTHIANS 9:6–15
PSALM 65   LUKE 17:11–19

Bless our Creator for the good land we have been given. For flowing streams and springs which water the ground, we give you thanks, O God. For the land which produces oats, barley, wheat, and soybeans, we offer our prayer with gratitude. For trees that produce beautiful flowers and delicious fruits, we delight in songs of thanksgiving. We thank you, O God, for the land where we may eat bread without scarcity and where we have more than enough for all.

Move us to be thoughtfully gracious with the bounty we are privileged to enjoy. Deliver us from a thoughtless neglect of prayers of thankfulness. Remove from us the attitude which struts around claiming that "by my power and by my might, I have forced the ground to produce bread for the sower." Restore in us a saving sense of gratitude for the beauty and bounty of the land you have given, Holy God.

As we enjoy your bounteous goodness, O God, move us to sow bountifully the spirit of generosity. Sustain in us the joy of cheerful giving. Guide our giving so that it may provide in abundance for every good work. Enrich in every way an increase in the harvest of good gifts given. Each day sustain us in the godly habit of self-forgetfulness in wondrous acts of kindness. Draw us near to you, O God, in a fellowship of thoughtful and appropriate giving.

Open all hearts, dear God, to delight in the bounty of your earth. As children dancing joyously in the fresh spring, allow us to skip in the meadows of your mercy. We shout and sing together for the joy of thanksgiving. Let the people with thankfulness say   *Amen.*

Dedication (or Rededication) of a Church

God of all times and places, we are eager to know you in *this* hour, in *this* house of worship built to honor you. Your presence fills this sanctuary. Your love is poured into our midst. Symbols of your care are all around us, in the design of this sacred space, but even more so in the people who gather here to experience your reality in songs of praise and the deep yearnings of prayer. Come, Holy Spirit, to live in us and among us and through us.

You have witnessed the pain and sacrifice that have marked the building of this church. You, O God, are aware of our disagreements, struggles, and anxiety. You know our anger and resentment against one another when things have not gone our way. Some feelings we have admitted openly. Others we have nursed quietly and still carry. All of them we bring to you today, seeking forgiveness. Release us from any lingering disharmony that we may with one voice glorify your holy name. Cleanse us from pride and possessiveness that we may eagerly share these hallowed halls with other seekers.

With joyous thanksgiving, we dedicate this spiritual home in your honor, Gracious God, and to the service of your whole human family. May it be a source of healing, feeding, comfort, and challenge as we work together toward the realization of your reign among us. Teach us to gather with expectation, to listen with openness and compassion, and to serve with diligence. Let your Word fill our words with truth and our lives with faithful response. Even in these moments, let each one in this assembly hear the call of Christ. Lead us to renewed self-dedication as this building is consecrated for the ministries you intend. All praise be to you, O God.   *Amen.*

Prayer on a Day Honoring Teachers

PROVERBS 22:6, 17–19   2 TIMOTHY 2:1–2, 14–15, 24–25a
PSALM 90:12–14, 16–17   MATTHEW 28:16–20

Almighty God, we gather today as a thankful people, grateful for generations of teachers who have told the stories of your love. We rejoice in everyone who has inclined an ear to you, seeking to discern your Word. We have heard their witness through the years. They have been good workers in our midst, daring to encounter and explain wisdom far beyond our full understanding.

We confess, Eternal One, that we have not always listened. When teachers have counseled obedience, we have been more likely to rebel. When they have suggested sacrifice, we have opted for safety. When they have summoned us to discipleship, we have fled from responsibility. We have preferred wrangling over working, autonomy rather than the authority of Christ, grumbling more than gratitude. Teachers have not had an easy time with us.

O God, your compassion has been well expressed in your servants. Your works are manifest in them. Your favor has rested on them, and through them, on us. In spite of our resistance, you have prospered their work. In their words and their lives, your call reaches our ears and our hearts. We present ourselves to you, for we are becoming disciples of Jesus Christ. We have heard your summons to teach others, to witness in deeds of patience and gentleness to the truth you are revealing to us.

Stretch our attention to embrace those you would have us teach. Temper our speech with active listening, our counsel with deep caring, our truth-seeking with openness to your continuing revelation. Grant us wise hearts and genuine faithfulness. Awaken us each day to your steadfast love that we may join in glad celebration with all who seek to serve you.   *Amen.*

Reflections

Reflections

Reflections

Reflections

Index of Scripture Readings

Old Testament

PROVERBS

22:6, 17—19 Prayers on a Day Honoring
Teachers

ECCLESIASTES

3:1—13 New Year's Day (A, B, C)

ISAIAH

2:1—5 First Sunday of Advent
2:1—5 Third Sunday of Advent
5:1—7 Proper 22
7:10—16 Fourth Sunday of Advent
9:1—4 Third Sunday after the Epiphany
9:2—7 Christmas Eve/Day—Proper 1
11:1—10 Second Sunday of Advent
25:1—9 Proper 23
25:6—9 Easter Evening
42:1—9 Baptism of Jesus
42:1—9 Monday of Holy Week
45:1—7 Proper 24
49:1—7 Second Sunday after the Epiphany
49:1—7 Tuesday of Holy Week
49:8—16 Eighth Sunday after the
   Epiphany
50:4—9 Sixth Sunday in Lent (Passion
   Sunday)
50:4—9 Wednesday of Holy Week
51:1—6 Proper 16
52:7—10 Christmas Day
52:13—53:12 Good Friday (A, B, C)
55:10—13 Proper 10
55:1—5 Proper 13
56:1, 6—8 Proper 15
58:1—9 Fifth Sunday after the Epiphany
58:1—12 Ash Wednesday
60:1—6 Epiphany of Jesus
62:6—12 Christmas Day
63:7—9 First Sunday after Christmas Day

JEREMIAH

15:15—21 Proper 17
20:7—13 Proper 7
28:5—9 Proper 8
31:1—6 Easter Day
31:7—14 Second Sunday after
   Christmas Day

LAMENTATIONS

3:1—9, 19—24 Holy Saturday

EZEKIEL

18:1—4, 25—32 Proper 21
33:7—11 Proper 18
34:11—16, 20—24 Proper 29
37:1—14 Fifth Sunday in Lent

HOSEA

5:15—6:16 Proper 5

JOEL

2:1—2, 12—17 Ash Wednesday

AMOS

5:18—27 Proper 27

JONAH

3:10—4:11 Proper 20

MICAH

3:5—12 Proper 26
6:1—8 Fourth Sunday after the Epiphany

MALACHI

3:1—4 Presentation

New Testament

MATTHEW

1:18—25 Fourth Sunday of Advent
2:1—12 Epiphany of Jesus
2:13—23 First Sunday after Christmas Day
3:1—12 Second Sunday of Advent
3:13—17 Baptism of Jesus
4:1—11 First Sunday in Lent
4:12—23 Third Sunday after the Epiphany
5:1—12 Fourth Sunday after the Epiphany
5:13—20 Fifth Sunday after the Epiphany
5:21—37 Sixth Sunday after the Epiphany
5:38—48 Seventh Sunday after the
   Epiphany
6:1—6, 16—21 Last Sunday after the
   Epiphany
6:24—34 Eighth Sunday after the
   Epiphany
7:21—29 Ninth Sunday after the Epiphany
7:21—27 Proper 4
9:9—13, 13—26 Proper 5
9:35, 10:8 Proper 6

10:24–39 Proper 7
10:40–42 Proper 8
11:16–19, 25–30 Proper 9
13:1–9, 18–23 Proper 10
14:24–30, 36–43 Proper 11
13:31–33 Proper 12
13:44–52 Proper 13
14:22–33 Proper 14
15:21–28 Proper 15
16:13–20 Proper 16
16:21–28 Proper 17
17:1–9 Last Sunday after the Epiphany
17:1–9 Second Sunday in Lent
18:15–20 Proper 18
18:21–35 Proper 19
20:1–16 Proper 20
21:23–32 Proper 21
21:33–46 Proper 22
22:1–14 Proper 23
22:15–22 Proper 24
22:34–46 Proper 25
23:1–12 Proper 26
24:36–44 First Sunday of Advent
25:1–13 Proper 27
25:14–30 Proper 28
25:31–46 Proper 29
25:31–46 New Year's Day (A, B, C)
26:14–27 Sixth Sunday in Lent
27:11–54 Passion Sunday (Sixth Sunday in Lent)
27:57–66 Holy Saturday (A, B, C)
28:1–10 Easter Day
28:1–10 Easter Day
28:16–20 Trinity Sunday
28:16–20 Prayer on a Day Honoring Teachers

LUKE
1:39–57 Visitation
2:1–14 Christmas Eve/Day—Proper 1
2:1–7, 8–20 Christmas Day—Proper 2 (A, B, C)
2:15–21 Holy Name of Jesus (A, B, C)
2:22–40 Presentation
17:11–19 Thanksgiving Day
24:13–49 Easter Evening
24:44–53 Ascension of Jesus

JOHN
1:1–9, 10–18 Second Sunday after Christmas Day

1:29–42 Second Sunday after the Epiphany
3:13–17 Holy Cross
3:1–17 Second Sunday in Lent
4:5–42 Third Sunday in Lent
9:1–41 Fourth Sunday in Lent
10:1–14 First Sunday after Christmas Day
10:1–10 Fourth Sunday of Easter
11:1–45 Fifth Sunday in Lent
12:1–11 Monday of Holy Week (A, B, C)
12:20–36 Tuesday of Holy Week (A, B, C)
13:1–17 Holy Thursday (A, B, C)
13:21–32 Wednesday of Holy Week (A, B, C)
14:1–14 Fifth Sunday of Easter
14:15–21 Sixth Sunday of Easter
17 Seventh Sunday of Easter
18:1–19:42 Good Friday (A, B, C)
20:1–18 Easter Day
20:19–31 Second Sunday of Easter
20:19–23 Day of Pentecost

ACTS
1:1–11 Ascension of Jesus
1:6–14 Seventh Sunday of Easter
2:1–21 Day of Pentecost
2:14–32 Second Sunday of Easter
2:14–41 Third Sunday of Easter
2:42–46 Fourth Sunday of Easter
7:55–60 Fifth Sunday of Easter
17:22–31 Sixth Sunday of Easter

ROMANS
1:1–7 Fourth Sunday of Advent
1:16–17; 3:22–28 Ninth Sunday after the Epiphany
4:1–5, 13–17 Second Sunday in Lent
4:13–25 Proper 5
5:12–19 First Sunday in Lent
5:1–11 Third Sunday in Lent
5:1–8 Proper 6
6:1–11 Proper 7
6:12–23 Proper 8
7:15–25 Proper 9
8:6–11 Fifth Sunday in Lent
8:1–11 Proper 10
8:12–25 Proper 11
8:26–39 Proper 12
9:1–5 Proper 13
10:5–15 Proper 14

Reflections

11:1–2, 29–32 Proper 15
12:1–8 Proper 16
12:9–21 Proper 17
12:9–16 Visitation
13:8–14 Proper 18
13:11–14 First Sunday of Advent
14:1–12 Proper 19
15:4–13 Second Sunday of Advent

1 CORINTHIANS
1:1–9 Second Sunday after the Epiphany
1:10–18 Third Sunday after the Epiphany
1:18–24 Holy Cross
1:18–31 Fourth Sunday after the
  Epiphany
1:18–31 Tuesday of Holy Week
  (A, B, C)
2:1–12 Fifth Sunday after the Epiphany
3:1–9 Sixth Sunday after the Epiphany
3:10–11, 16–23 Seventh Sunday after the
  Epiphany
4:1–5 Eighth Sunday after the Epiphany
11:23–26 Holy Thursday (A, B, C)
12:3a–13 Day of Pentecost
24:13–49 Easter Evening

2 CORINTHIANS
5:20 Ash Wednesday (A, B, C)
9:6–15 Thanksgiving Day
13:11–13 Trinity Sunday

GALATIANS
4:4–7 Holy Name of Jesus (A, B, C)

EPHESIANS
1:3–14 Second Sunday after Christmas
  Day (A, B, C)
1:15–23 Ascension of Jesus
1:15–23 Proper 29
3:1–12 Epiphany of Jesus (A, B, C)
5:8–14 Fourth Sunday in Lent

PHILIPPIANS
1:21–30 Proper 20
2:5–11 Sixth Sunday in Lent (Passion
  Sunday)
2:1–13 Proper 21

3:4–14 Proper 22
4:1–9 Proper 23

1 THESSALONIANS
1:1–10 Proper 24
2:1–8 Proper 25
2:9–13 Proper 26
4:13–18 Proper 27
5:1–11 Proper 28

2 TIMOTHY
2:1–2, 14–15, 24–15a Prayers on a Day
  Honoring Teachers

TITUS
2:1–14, 15–20 Christmas Eve/Day—
  Proper 1 (A, B, C)
3:4–7 Christmas Day—Proper 2 (A, B, C)

HEBREWS
1:1–4 (5–12) Christmas Day—Proper 3
  (A, B, C)
2:10–18 First Sunday after Christmas Day
2:14–18 Presentation
9:11–15 Monday of Holy Week (A, B, C)
10:16–25 Good Friday (A, B, C)
12:1–3 Wednesday of Holy Week
  (A, B, C)

1 PETER
1:3–9 Second Sunday of Easter
1:17–23 Third Sunday of Easter
2:19–25 Fourth Sunday of Easter
2:2–10 Fifth Sunday of Easter
3:13–22 Sixth Sunday of Easter
4:12–14; 5:6–11 Seventh Sunday of
  Easter

2 PETER
1:16–21 Last Sunday after the Epiphany
  (Transfiguration Sunday)

1 JOHN
3:1–3 All Saints'

REVELATION
7:9–17 All Saints'
21:1–6 New Year's Day (A, B, C)